# THE PEANUT ALLERGY ANSWER BOOK

SECOND EDITION

# THE PEANUT ALLERGY ANSWER BOOK

## SECOND EDITION

Michael C. Young, M.D.

FAIR WINDS
PRESS
BEVERLY, MASSACHUSETTS

Text © 2001, 2006 by Michael C. Young, M.D.

First published in the USA in 2006 by
Fair Winds Press, a member of
Quayside Publishing Group
100 Cummings Center
Suite 406-L
Beverly, MA 01915

First edition 2001
Second edition 2006

10 09                    3 4 5

ISBN 13: 978-1-59233-233-1
ISBN 10: 1-59233-233-5

Library of Congress Cataloging-in-Publication Data available

Book design by *tabula rasa* graphic design

Printed and bound in USA

*This book is not intended to replace the services of a
physician. Any application of the recommendations set
forth in the following pages is at the reader's discretion.
The reader should consult with his or her own physician
or specialist concerning the recommendations in this book.*

This book is dedicated to my loving wife and daughter and to my father, who have provided me with their encouragement, inspiration, and love.

I also dedicate this book to the loving memory of my mother, who gave up her career as a young physician to raise my sister and me, and inspired us to the call of medicine and learning.

And to all who have food allergies, and to the dedicated people who work hard to make this world a safer place for them, you inspire and humble me. I dedicate this book to you.

# CONTENTS

CHAPTER 3

ANAPHYLAXIS

CHAPTER 4

PEANUT EXPOSURES

CHAPTER 5

FINDING THE HIDDEN PEANUT PRODUCTS

CHAPTER 6

KEEPING SAFE IN A PEANUT-FILLED WORLD

# ACKNOWLEDGMENTS

One of the true pleasures of practicing the specialty of allergy is having patients who are genuinely interested in finding out the causes and triggers of their problems rather than just treatments and cures. Allergy patients are interested in learning about their problems and how to prevent them. Over the years, I have had the privilege of caring for many patients and their families. I have learned much from all of them, and they are directly responsible for this book. I would like to extend my deepest gratitude to all of my patients.

In particular, I would like to thank Christopher Smith, once a peanut-allergic toddler, and his mother, Lisa Lavieri, who looked for a book on peanut allergy and was unable to find one. She discussed her search with her sister, Holly Schmidt, publisher at Fair Winds Press, who then contacted me to write this book. I owe Christopher, his mom, and his Aunt Holly special thanks. Particularly satisfying to me is that, since the publication of the first edition of this book, Christopher has outgrown his peanut allergy and is now a healthy eight-year-old.

I gratefully acknowledge and thank all of my teachers and colleagues, especially my mentors during my allergy fellowship training at Boston Children's Hospital, Drs. Raif Geha, Donald Leung, and Frank Twarog, and Martin Broff, who gave me the opportunity to join his practice. I also thank my colleagues for reviewing the first edition of this book and giving helpful comments and suggestions: Drs. S. Allan Bock, Martin D. Broff, Raif S. Geha, Donald Leung, James Rosen, Hugh Sampson, John S. Saryan, Lynda Schneider, Albert L. Sheffer, Frank Twarog, and Dale Umetsu.

I have a special word of thanks to Anne Muñoz-Furlong. Founder of the Food Allergy & Anaphylaxis Network (FAAN), she is the model of what a dedicated parent can do. She has single-handedly revolutionized the field of food allergy by forming the most important organization in the field of food allergy and by serving patients, the medical community, and the general public. For her achievements, Anne was awarded the Distinguished Layperson Award in 2000 by the American Academy of Allergy, Asthma and Immunology. I am privileged to have Anne review this book, assist me with her many helpful and thoughtful comments, and write the foreword. If my patients gave me purpose in writing this book, Anne gave me inspiration. I gratefully acknowledge her contributions to this book as well as to all people with food allergies. I also wish to thank Terry Furlong and Chris Weiss of FAAN, who contributed to the section on airlines and peanut allergy.

I thank Holly Schmidt, my publisher at Fair Winds Press, who not only gave me the opportunity to write this book but who, with her patient teaching, greatly improved my writing and helped shape this book in its early stages of development. I also thank Wendy Gardner, my editor, who provided assistance for the second edition of this book, as did John Gettings, managing editor, Alexis Sullivan, editorial assistant, Lauren Rubenzahl, copyeditor, and Kristy Mulkern, proofreader.

I acknowledge my dedicated nursing and office staff, and my associates, Drs. Martin D. Broff, Catherine O'Brien, and Marge Vallen for their support and friendship.

Finally, I thank my family, especially my wife Karen and my daughter Liane, whose understanding and love provide me with the inspiration for all that I do.

# FOREWORD

The incidence of food allergy is continuing on an upward trend, with an estimated 11 million Americans now believed to be allergic to common foods such as milk, eggs, peanuts, wheat, soy, fish, shellfish, and tree nuts. One study reported a doubling of peanut allergy in children in the past decade. Since the first edition of *The Peanut Allergy Answer Book* was published, we've acquired even more knowledge about food allergies, thanks to the many research studies and public policy changes that have occurred.

Awarded the 2005 Mariel C. Furlong Award for Making a Difference by The Food Allergy & Anaphylaxis Network, Dr. Michael Young continues to devote his time to caring for patients and providing them with the educational reference tools they need to better manage their peanut allergy.

Dr. Young has combined his unique perspective as a clinician and writer to bring us a book that is as easy for teens and adults to read and reference. The second edition of *The Peanut Allergy Answer Book* provides readers with cutting-edge information about peanut allergy, including the new research findings from school nurses, prevalence studies, and fatalities, as well as information about the first new self-injectible epinephrine for patients in twenty years. Dr. Young has presented the insight he's gained from his many presentations to parents and health care professionals; addressed commonly asked questions, concerns, and myths; and incorporated them into this latest edition.

If you thought the first edition was useful, this one surpasses it! Be sure that anyone who should have the latest in peanut allergy information has a copy of Dr. Young's useful new reference book.

*Anne Muñoz-Furlong*
*Founder and CEO*
*The Food Allergy & Anaphylaxis Network*

# PREFACE
# TO THE SECOND EDITION

Since the publication of *The Peanut Allergy Answer Book* five years ago, there has been much additional research published in the field of peanut allergy and anaphylaxis. This continues to be one of the most active areas in the specialty of allergy and immunology. For this new edition, I reviewed more than 250 new scientific publications on peanut allergy alone, including studies on the underlying mechanisms of how allergic reactions occur; promising new medicines and vaccines for treatment, management, and prevention of peanut allergy and anaphylaxis; new diagnostic tests; new information on the natural history of this allergy; and studies on the risks and management of different types of exposures to peanuts.

In the past five years, as the prevalence of peanut allergy has doubled in young children, public awareness of the societal impact of peanut allergy has greatly increased. More and more peanut-allergic infants and toddlers are entering daycares, preschools, and schools. This trend has led to the publication of guidelines for schools in managing food allergies and anaphylaxis, the enactment of the Food Allergen Labeling and Consumer Protection Act (effective January 1, 2006), pending legislation on national guidelines for school policies on the safe management of food allergies in schools, and proposed legislation for national restaurant guidelines for food-allergic consumers. Many of these strides have been due to the huge effort of the Food Allergy & Anaphylaxis Network, which advocates for all food-allergic patients, educating schools, communities, and the lay public by not only funding scientific and clinical research (including a global symposium on anaphylaxis) but by actively conducting research studies and supporting local, state, and national legislative efforts to make the world a safer place for people with food allergies.

However, despite all these accomplishments, despite increased scientific knowledge and understanding, and despite schools and communities working harder to protect and safeguard peanut-allergic children, anaphylactic reactions continue to occur and, tragically, fatal food reactions have not decreased. The role of information and education in this area of medicine has never been more important. Our work is not finished!

I wrote this book to bring together all of the available information necessary to understand and manage this important medical problem in an easy-to-read question-and-answer format. Returning readers will find that the original material has been updated and revised and will discover almost 50 percent new information in this second edition. The bibliography has been updated with many new references and studies so that you can refer to the original sources for more information. I encourage you to use the table of contents for any specific questions you might have. You do not have to read this book in sequential order; many readers refer to the specific questions (i.e., chapters) as they arise over time or just browse through the questions that interest them. There is also a lot of useful information for people allergic to foods other than peanuts. Much of the general information can be applied to you as well.

I wish to thank the many readers of the first edition for their very helpful comments and suggestions; you are the inspiration for this second edition. As knowledge increases and progress continues in the coming years, I will continue to update and revise *The Peanut Allergy Answer Book* for future editions.

# INTRODUCTION

The number of peanut-allergic people I treat as an allergist has dramatically increased in the past few years. Where I might have routinely seen four or five patients a week with peanut allergy just five years ago, I now often see more than five or six a day for the same problem. Most of the people with peanut allergy I treated fifteen or more years ago were adults; today, my peanut-allergic patients—particularly those with new peanut allergies—are exclusively very young children and infants. The number of people, especially young children, with life-threatening allergic reactions has also dramatically increased. There has been heightened interest in peanut allergy, especially with the recent focus on banning peanuts from schools and airlines.

There are numerous explanations for the increasing numbers of peanut-allergic people. One is the very high level of consumption of peanuts and peanut products all over the world. More than five billion pounds of peanuts are produced each year in the U.S. alone, more than any other country. According to the United States Peanut Council, eleven pounds of peanut products are ingested annually by the average American. About 55 percent is consumed in the form of peanut butter, and the remainder is consumed as table nuts and in baked goods and candies. Peanuts and peanut products, especially peanut butter, are inexpensive and convenient food sources and have become very popular as snacks and quick meals, often standing in for regular full meals in many busy households. Infants and young children become exposed to peanut products very early in life. The result of this increased exposure to peanuts and peanut products is that the number of people allergic to peanuts has greatly increased in the past ten years. Peanut allergy is unfortunately a potentially life-threatening allergy and, for most children who have it, a lifelong problem.

When Holly Schmidt, my publisher at Fair Winds Press, first approached me to write this book, I was surprised to learn that there were no books available specifically on the subject of peanut allergy. From the large numbers of patients I follow in my private practice in Massachusetts and in the Allergy Clinic at Boston Children's Hospital, I knew that there was a need for a comprehensive book on this subject. This book is written for the increasing number of people with peanut allergies and their families. It addresses the many issues they face, from knowing what foods contain peanut and peanut products to performing emergency planning in the event of a life-threatening allergic attack.

I have tried to make medical terms easy to understand. Use the glossary in the back of the book for new terms. Many of these new words are bold-faced in the text.

From reading this book, you will learn how to prevent and manage peanut allergy successfully and thus will not have to live in constant fear of life-threatening exposures. You will learn all you need to know about peanuts and allergies and will be able to design strategies to cope with this allergy.

# CHAPTER 1

# ALLERGIES IN A NUTSHELL

### What is food allergy?

Matthew is a six-month-old baby who has been breast-fed since birth. At two months of age, his mother introduced rice cereal into his diet with no problems. Subsequently, she gave him oatmeal and applesauce, and at five months of age, he had egg for the first time. He developed on his face a very itchy dry scaly rash that, over the course of several weeks, worsened to involve the creases of his arms, the backs of the knees, and his neck and ears. His pediatrician diagnosed "baby eczema" and prescribed a moisturizer and hydrocortisone cream.

---

The rash improved, but it did not resolve. It seemed to worsen with food, but there was no consistent pattern. When his mother brought him to my office, allergy tests showed he was allergic to milk, soy, egg white, wheat, and peanut. His rash significantly improved with the elimination of these foods from his diet.

The symptoms of food allergy in children typically involve the skin. Hives are common, particularly on areas of contact such as the mouth, lips, and face, and in severe cases, these areas can become swollen and intensely itchy. When the skin becomes chronically inflamed, the rashes take the form of eczema, a very itchy, dry, scaly eruption that often begins in early infancy. Typical areas of skin involvement are the face, arms, and legs, particularly the creases, which include knees, elbows, neck, and behind the ears.

Gastrointestinal symptoms are also common, ranging from nausea, vomiting, and diarrhea to acute severe abdominal pain and colic. More subtle reactions can take the form of failure to eat and gain weight.

Respiratory symptoms, such as wheezing, nasal congestion, and mucous secretion, are less common chronically but can be severe when they occur. Some people with asthma have food allergy, and their asthma can be triggered by the ingestion of the foods to which they are sensitized. Conversely, some people with food allergy who do not have asthma can experience an asthma-like reaction when they eat the foods they're allergic to. When these people are studied, they often have an asthmatic tendency, although their baseline lung function is usually normal. That is, although they do not have the diagnosis of asthma, they may be prone to chest symptoms such as chronic cough or wheezing with common colds, physical activity, and exercise.

Finally, anaphylaxis, which is a life-threatening systemic allergic reaction, can occur. It is rare but is, of course, the most dangerous of all allergic reactions and what we all work to prevent and avoid.

Food allergy is more common in children than in adults. It has been estimated that 6 to 8 percent of infants younger than age two are allergic to food, and approximately 1.5 percent of adults have food allergy. The common food allergens for children are milk, eggs, soy, wheat, peanuts, nuts, and seafood. Of these, milk, eggs and peanuts cause 80 percent of all food allergies in children. In adults, the common food allergens are tree nuts, peanut, fish, and shellfish, which cause 85 percent of allergic reactions. A recent survey in the U.S. suggests that 1.2 percent of children are allergic to peanuts and tree nuts. Sensitivity to many foods, especially milk, eggs and soy, tend to resolve with age, whereas allergy to peanuts and tree nuts often begins in infancy but fails to improve with age. For reasons that are still unclear, peanut allergy is associated with fatal anaphylaxis more than any other food.

Food allergies usually occur in individuals who also have other manifestations of allergic disease, such as hay fever, asthma, and eczema. People with these disorders have a greater tendency to develop sensitivities to food. Because allergies tend to be inherited, family members are often allergic as well, although not necessarily in the same ways. Although allergies to specific foods are not inherited per se, the general tendency to be allergic to food is genetic. Some recent studies now suggest the possibility of genetic transmission of peanut allergy.

### What is food allergy and how does it relate to the immune system?

Richard is a forty-three-year-old man who had milk allergy as a child and was affected by eczema and chronic diarrhea. On a milk-and-dairy-free diet, he eventually outgrew these symptoms and was able to consume milk products by the time he entered school. He had no further allergy problems until he developed hay fever and asthma at age thirteen. These symptoms remain unchanged and are usually worse in the spring, when the trees pollinate; he also has hives and wheezing when he is near cats and dogs. His two-year-old son, who has chronic eczema and recurrent ear infections, recently developed hives from exposure to peanut butter.

---

People commonly think of allergies as the sneezing; itchy, watery eyes; and stuffy noses that occur when they get "hay fever" in the spring and fall. Some other people wheeze and have trouble breathing from asthma attacks when they exercise or when they "feel allergic." Still others become deathly ill when they are stung by bees and yellow jackets. How do all of these different problems relate to the person who is unable to eat certain foods, such as peanuts or shellfish, because they break out in hives, experience swelling of their throat, or have abdominal pain and diarrhea?

These reactions are all results of the body's immune system reacting in an inappropriate way to what should be innocent and innocuous things in our daily lives. That is what an allergy is. In order to understand how this happens, we need to learn a little bit about how our immune system works and how it can cause us to get allergies to different things. We will also learn the definition of a few key words, such as allergen, IgE, mast cells, and histamine.

The immune system is responsible for protecting the human body from infection and invasion by bacteria, viruses, and other harmful agents. It accomplishes the goal through its ability to distinguish "self" from "nonself." Substances identified as foreign, or "nonself," are attacked by cells of the immune system and destroyed or rendered inactive.

The immune system in allergic people is different from that of nonallergic individuals in it identifies innocuous and benign things, such as food, pollen, animal dander, and medications, as harmful to the body and targets them for an immune response. This response is a very potent inflammatory reaction that results from the production of a special protein called **IgE,** which recognizes a specific allergic agent (**allergen**) in the same way that antibodies recognize bacteria and viruses. This recognition is very specific because a given IgE protein is unique to one and only one allergen. So, peanut-specific IgE will recognize only peanut, and cat-specific IgE will recognize only cat. This is the reason why some people are allergic to certain things but not to others: A person with peanut-specific IgE will react to peanuts only and not to cat, unless he or she also has cat-specific IgE.

IgE proteins circulate in our bloodstream throughout our whole body and find their way to various tissues and organs, such as the skin, gastrointestinal tract, lungs, nose, and eyes. Upon reaching these areas, the IgE attaches to cells called **mast cells,** which are located in these organs and tissues, and you become "sensitized" to that particular allergen. Mast cells are important in allergies because they make the chemical **histamine,** as well as other chemical **mediators.** Histamine is the chemical that directly causes the many symptoms of allergies, such as itching, hives, stuffy nose, and wheezing. When the sensitized tissues come in contact with the allergen—through ingestion or inhalation, for example—the allergen attaches to the tissues by means of the allergen-specific IgE mast cell complex. This attachment causes the mast cell to release large amounts of histamine and other similar chemical mediators into the blood. Histamine circulates through the blood and to surrounding tissues and subsequently binds to these tissues by means of histamine receptors.

We use **antihistamine** medications to block the actions of histamine, thereby blocking allergic symptoms. Antihistamines work by inhibiting the binding of histamine to these tissue receptors.

Histamine binding results in many tissue reactions and changes. In the nose and eyes, congestion, swelling, mucous secretion, itching, and sneezing result. In the lungs, constriction of air passages results in shortness of breath, wheezing, and difficulty breathing. In the gastrointestinal tract, vomiting, diarrhea, and abdominal cramping result. In the skin, itching, swelling, hives, and eczema result. In the most severe reaction, the cardiovascular system is affected, with a drop in blood pressure, shock, and potentially death. This potentially fatal reaction is called **anaphylaxis.** Allergic reactions in which more than one organ system is involved, such as symptoms of both hives and wheezing or both itchy throat and vomiting, is also anaphylaxis.

The allergens that are the most common causes of life-threatening anaphylaxis are those that are absorbed into the body internally, such as food, medications, insect stings, and, in certain instances, latex rubber. Of the foods, the most potent allergens are peanuts, tree nuts, fish, and shellfish. These are the foods most commonly associated with anaphylaxis, and of these, peanut is number one on the list. The treatment and prevention of anaphylaxis will be discussed in later chapters.

### How do you know if you have a food allergy?

I have always loved all kinds of seafood, especially shellfish. I was attending a meeting of allergists and had just returned to my hotel room following a delicious buffet luncheon where quite a bit of seafood had been served and where, following my appetite, I had indulged myself, especially in the lobster and crab dishes. I noticed that my entire chest and abdomen were suddenly intensely itchy and hot. I noted on my watch that approximately thirty minutes had gone by since I had finished lunch. I took off my shirt and was surprised to see myself covered in large red hives. I looked in the mirror and saw that my entire body was bright red. At this time, I also felt my heart racing and a tightness in my throat. "This must be what early anaphylaxis feels like!" I thought. I had never felt this way before. Luckily, I had some antihistamine samples I had gotten earlier in the meeting. I took two tablets and tried not to panic. After all, I was at an allergy meeting full of allergists! Surely, someone must have epinephrine!

Fortunately, the itching and hives started to recede, and after a long hour, I felt much better but quite sleepy from the side effects of the antihistamine. I missed the rest of the meeting that day. The following morning, my allergist colleagues asked me where I was. Apparently, I had missed an interesting lecture on food allergies! Later that week, when I returned to work, I skin-tested myself with our panel of common allergenic foods. I had a positive skin test to crabmeat only and was negative to everything else. In the six years since that incident, I have meticulously avoided crabmeat but have eaten all other shellfish and seafood with no problems. I recently repeated the skin test to crabmeat, and it was negative. Subsequently, I have resumed eating crabmeat with no problems.

Food allergies are usually recognized initially by the person or the person's family. Allergic symptoms such as itching, hives, eczema, abdominal pain, nausea, vomiting, diarrhea, and breathing difficulty are all common symptoms of food allergy. When the symptoms occur in a consistent and recognizable pattern—that is, following the ingestion of a specific food—it becomes obvious that food allergy may be the cause of the various symptoms.

For example, ingestion of peanuts can result in the immediate eruption of hives, swelling, and difficulty breathing. This reaction is not subtle, and you can make the diagnosis easily. When the symptoms are chronic and inconsistent, however, it may be less clear whether the cause is a specific individual food or several foods, or perhaps not even to food at all.

Seeing an allergy specialist to diagnose or document suspected food allergy may be very helpful. The allergist can sort through confusing symptoms and make deductions and conclusions based on your history. He or she also can perform allergy testing to confirm the presence of specific food allergies.

### How do I choose an allergist?

An allergist specializes in the diagnosis and treatment of allergic diseases and asthma. Allergists complete an additional six years of specialty training after receiving their medical degree. An allergist needs to complete training and pass the board examinations in either internal medicine or pediatrics before being allowed to take the allergy board examination. Allergy specialty training consists of three additional years of training in allergy and immunology in fellowship programs, during which the doctor will learn about how to diagnose and treat hay fever, asthma, eczema, food, drug, and insect allergies in children and adults. Choosing a board-certified allergist will ensure that your doctor has completed the required allergy and immunology training and passed the examination for the allergy specialty.

Your primary care physician is the best person to contact regarding a referral to the best local allergist for you. Your primary care physician would have an established relationship with that doctor and know his or her particular style and expertise with allergy patients. Your doctor may know the allergy specialist's particular interests, which may include food allergies. The American Academy of Allergy, Asthma and Immunology (www.AAAAI.org) and the American College of Allergy, Asthma and Immunology (www.ACAAI.org) are national organizations of allergy specialists, and they can give you names of all the allergists in your local area. Other organizations that can help with referrals to allergists are the local chapters of the American Lung Association and the Allergy and Asthma Foundation of America, as well as your local medical society.

As when selecting any adviser, first meet the allergist and talk to him or her to determine whether there is compatibility, compassion, and trust. A good doctor will above all *listen* to you and allow you to speak freely about your problem and all of your concerns regarding it. The art of good medicine is to be able to take a good history from the patient, and you can tell a lot about the doctor's knowledge from his or her questions. Frequently, good questions can help you to think about the problem better, and ultimately you might be able to come up with answers yourself.

If you are a parent, observe how the doctor relates to the child and whether a rapport develops. Never underestimate the ability of a child to describe his or her observations—a good doctor experienced with children can elicit this history effectively, even from small children.

Regardless of whether you're the patient or the patient's parent, go to the doctor's appointment with a specific list of questions and concerns. Everything seems more confused and hectic during the appointment, so having something concrete to refer to will make things much smoother and easier.

## What information does your doctor need to diagnose food allergy?

*Doctor, I have food allergies!*

Please describe your symptoms.

*I have nausea and pain in my stomach every time I eat.*

Have you noticed which foods cause these symptoms?

*I can't really tell. It seems that all meals will do it.*

How soon after you eat do you feel the nausea and stomach pain?

*Sometimes it's during the meal, and other times it's a few hours afterwards.*

Do you have any other symptoms along with the nausea and pain, such as itching, hives, swelling, or difficulty breathing or swallowing?

*Yes, but I get those all the time, not just with eating!*

---

Food allergy symptoms can be very difficult to sort through, and often the symptoms are very vague and nonspecific in nature, which makes them difficult for you and your doctor to diagnose. The key to solving this puzzle is a history carefully taken by an allergist or a physician with experience in dealing with food allergies. The physician will take a detailed history of your symptoms, paying special attention to the sequence of reactions and correlating the timing of your symptoms with the specific foods eaten. Severely allergic people usually experience their reactions within thirty to sixty minutes after they eat. Delayed symptoms sometimes occur as well, which can make it more difficult to determine which food is the cause of the reaction. In this situation, the consistency and pattern of responses can help clarify what is going on.

## What are allergy tests?

The suspicion of food allergy can be verified using allergy tests, which are usually performed by an allergy specialist. The allergist has specialized training and certification in the treatment of allergic and immunologic diseases, including the diagnosis and management of food allergies, and is best able to interpret the results of allergy testing. Documentation of specific food allergies can be done by either **skin prick tests** or IgE **RAST** tests by blood sampling.

## The Food Diary

One of the most useful tools in the diagnosis of food allergy, for both the doctor and the patient, is a carefully kept journal in which you record your exact symptoms (e.g., itching, hives, nausea, abdominal pain, trouble breathing, etc.), the timing of the first symptoms in relation to meals and eating, and, most importantly, a complete list of everything eaten. Ideally, this list should include all food and drink items, as well as the ingredient lists of processed foods. The reason to keep such a list is that, as we'll learn later in this book, there are many "hidden foods and ingredients" contained in products. Artificial flavoring, dyes, and preservatives can cause allergic reactions in some people.

Recording how much of the food you eat is important, especially the smallest amount that will cause a reaction. The most recent reaction as well as the number of times that a reaction has occurred with each food is also helpful. Review of this information can provide great insight into whether specific foods are responsible for specific symptoms. Often, hidden sources of exposure, such as cross-contamination, can be deduced from a carefully recorded food diary. Food diaries also can be helpful in assessing chronic conditions, such as eczema or chronic gastroenteritis, in which acute exacerbations and attacks may be rare.

### Kinds

*Skin Testing*

In skin testing, a very dilute extract of the actual food is used. The allergenic extract material is processed and purified by commercial laboratories. A drop of the liquid extract is placed on the skin; a plastic or metal point is then used to prick the skin just enough for the extract material to penetrate but not actually break the skin. If the person is allergic to the extract material, his or her skin mast cells will already be sensitized to it and the person will have a histamine-mediated reaction. That is, the histamine will cause a small hive where the skin was pricked in the skin test.

When performing skin tests, your allergist also will administer a positive control with histamine to demonstrate that the skin is capable of reacting. The normal skin response of all people is to have a reaction to histamine with some itching, redness, and a small hive. In some situations, however, the skin response to histamine is blocked or diminished, and the skin would not respond to any allergen testing. The most common situation in which the histamine response is absent occurs when you have taken antihistamine medication before the skin tests. For that reason, be sure to stop antihistamine medications five to seven days prior to skin tests; otherwise, your histamine response, as well as your response to any potential allergen tests, may be blocked.

Your doctor will also administer a negative control with saline (a salt water solution) to control for the possibility of false positive skin tests caused by certain sensitive skin conditions. Skin tests can be read in twenty minutes and are inexpensive and minimally uncomfortable, with minor itching being the main effect. In children younger than two years, the skin may not always be reactive, and false negative skin tests may result. Some doctors suggest that, in the case of a negative skin test, the skin test be repeated, using a fresh sample of the actual food, as there may be loss of activity or potency in the manufacturing process of the extract material.

*IgE RAST Tests*

Blood tests used to diagnose allergies are referred to as RAST (radioallergosorbent) tests. The original technique involved radioactive reagents, but most laboratories currently use non-radioactive "tracers" that rely on color changes in the reagents.

The test works by detecting the presence of allergen specific IgE in your blood. In it, your blood is drawn from the arm and sent to the laboratory, where it is processed. This processing involves adding your blood to the allergen that has been attached to a paper disc, plastic plate, or cellulose matrix. After a timed interval, this mixture is washed and a "tracer" anti-IgE antibody is added to detect the binding of your IgE to the allergen. The amount of allergen-specific IgE contained in your blood sample can be calculated from this result. How high, or positive, the RAST test is reflects how much antibody you have to that specific allergen.

Although the RAST test is less accurate than skin prick tests, it can be useful in people who are unable to stop antihistamine therapy, people who have extensive skin disease, or people who have a significant risk of anaphylaxis from the skin testing. The main problem with RAST tests is that the results can vary considerably from laboratory to laboratory due to differences in laboratory technique, procedure, and quality control.

Recently, a modified type of RAST test, called the CAP RAST system, has been shown to more accurately measure the degree of allergy. This system correlates with the outcomes of double-blinded-placebo-controlled food challenges for four foods in particular: peanut, milk, egg, and fish. The CAP RAST levels are measured in units called kU/L and range from 0.35 to 100. The levels of allergen-specific IgE measured by the CAP system correlate with how active your symptoms are, and if these levels decline, it may indicate that you are losing the allergy.

This test may be a better way of following food allergies, since skin tests can remain positive even when clinical activity lessens as a child "outgrows" the food allergy. I recommend the new CAP RAST system over the older RAST test for doing allergy testing by blood sample, particularly if you are interested in following the course of the food allergy over time. Most, but not all, hospital and commercial laboratories now use the CAP RAST system for measuring allergy blood tests. If your test results are not in the kU/L units, the test was not done by the CAP RAST method. You can have your doctor check to see whether your local lab uses this method.

### Do allergy tests predict the severity of a reaction?

No. Neither skin prick tests nor CAP RAST tests will predict the severity of a reaction to any given exposure to peanut. The skin test and CAP RAST test do however, indicate the activity of the allergy. That is, the larger the skin test diameter and the higher the RAST level, the more "active" the allergy is, the more likely a reaction will occur on exposure, and the less likely you are to outgrow or resolve your peanut allergy.

Dr. Hugh Sampson, a prominent investigator in field of food allergy and director of The Jaffe Food Allergy Institute at New York's Mt. Sinai School of Medicine, found that if your peanut CAP RAST level was 15 kU/L or greater, you would have a 95 percent chance of reacting to peanut on a challenge. However, even though the likelihood of a reaction will be high, the actual reaction symptoms can be mild, moderate, severe, or even fatal and are not predictable by testing. The reaction to any given exposure depends on many different factors, such as the amount of exposure, the route of exposure (e.g., ingestion vs. skin contact), and your health status at the time of exposure (e.g., whether you have active allergy and asthma symptoms).

Thus, the adjectives often designated by each RAST level, such as "mild" or "severe," are completely misleading and serve no purpose. They are arbitrary, and because RAST levels do not predict the severity of reactions, these adjectives are meaningless and should be ignored.

In the future, a blood test may be able to predict the severity of clinical reactions, as well as how likely the allergy is to be outgrown. In 2004, Dr. Hugh Sampson and his colleagues published a new laboratory test called a microarray immunoassay (MIA), which measures the amount of IgE binding to epitopes, regions of the peanut protein that attach to the patient's IgE. The structure of the peanut protein's epitopes have been found to correlate with the severity of reactions, as well as how permanent the allergy can be. The amount of binding of a patient's peanut-specific IgE to certain epitopes of the peanut protein, and the total amount of binding in this MIA blood test, correlated with severe reactions and the likelihood of outgrowing the peanut allergy. This MIA test is still under investigation and is not yet available, but it holds much promise for the future management of peanut allergy.

### How accurate are allergy tests?

The accuracy of an allergy test is determined by how often it correctly predicts that a reaction will occur when you are exposed to that allergen. There is always a range of accuracy for any test. When a test is positive but you have no problems being exposed to that allergen, the test is said to be a "false positive." If, on the other hand, a test is negative but you get reactions from that allergen, the test is "falsely negative." For food allergies, tests can be falsely positive more than 50 percent of the time! On the other hand, the rate of false negative tests is much lower, particularly with skin tests.

False positive allergy tests are often caused by similarities in proteins that may be found in foods belonging to the same food family. For example, because peanuts and soy both belong to the legume family, there are similarities in the protein structures of both plants, and these similarities can cause the tests for both peanut and soy to turn positive. Peanut-allergic patients who do not have problems with eating soy often have positive test results for both foods even though actual clinical reactions only occur with peanut. In fact, 90 percent of peanut-allergic patients can eat soy.

### If I am eating peanuts with no problem and my allergy tests are positive for peanut, should I stop eating them?

If you are already eating peanuts and nuts and are not having any problems, you are not allergic to them, and there is no need to do allergy testing for peanut and nuts. If you have already been tested for peanut allergy despite having no problems eating peanuts, and the tests come back positive, you can disregard these false positive results and continue eating peanuts. Allergy testing done on a screening basis, without any preceding history of definite reactions to that food, can result in false positive tests that are clinically irrelevant and actually cause much confusion and unnecessary elimination of foods that have been well tolerated. Random allergy testing of the general population without regard to any clinical history generally results in positive tests five to six percent of the time.

In ordering allergy tests, the doctor must base his or her test selection on your clinical history. I do not generally order screening panels of foods except in the case of childhood eczema, which is often associated with food allergies, most commonly egg. Children with eczema often do not have a clear history of specific food triggers. If there are positive allergy tests, a trial of eliminating the positive foods, starting with the ones with the highest CAP RAST levels or largest skin tests, and careful observation of any improvement in the eczema can distinguish the clinically relevant foods from the false positives. If the results are unclear, I would recommend an oral food challenge as the next step.

### What is a food challenge?

Ultimately, the only way to know whether a food will cause a reaction is to actually eat it and see what happens. If eating the food consistently causes symptoms, then that food is a problem. If elimination of the food eliminates the symptoms you are having, that food would certainly be suspect. Using an elimination and challenge procedure is a practical way of testing your suspicions regarding any suspect foods that may be causing you problems.

When eliminating a food from your diet results in improvement and then eating it again causes your symptoms to recur, it is a problem food that should be avoided. This elimination and challenge procedure can be used to test suspect food allergies. However, if the symptoms are severe, such as swelling or difficulty with breathing or swallowing, this procedure is too dangerous to do on your own. Especially for foods commonly associated with anaphylaxis, such as peanuts, nuts, and seafood, it is best to undergo testing and possible challenge procedures under your doctor's supervision in his or her office, clinic, or hospital so that your safety is never compromised.

An oral food challenge consists of giving a very small amount of the food and then increasing amounts every fifteen to twenty minutes while watching for any signs of an allergic reaction. The procedure is stopped at the first sign of any allergic symptom. If there are no symptoms, the amount of food administered is increased up to an amount comparable to a real-life portion, such as a tablespoon amount. To eliminate any biases on the part of the patient or the doctor, the challenge can be "single-blinded" for the patient or "double-blinded" for both the patient and the doctor.

The definitive method of diagnosing food allergy is the **double-blind placebo-controlled food challenge (DBPCFC)**. It is useful to understand the DBPCFC method because it is referred to frequently in the food allergy literature. The DBPCFC is a functional test that seeks to reproduce the patient's actual symptoms by direct challenge. Therefore, it can be useful in the diagnosis of non-IgE mediated food reactions, such as lactose intolerance, as well as classical food allergies. The DBPCFC method eliminates the possibility of patient bias and investigator bias by "blinding" both sides so that neither the patient nor the physician knows whether the actual food or a placebo (i.e., a dummy sample that contains no food protein) is being given. There are many symptoms and reactions that can be mistaken for food-allergic reactions, so it is important to be able to objectively assess and separate these reactions from true allergic reactions.

To illustrate this concept, Dr. K. Rix and his colleagues in Great Britain studied twenty-three patients with a history of food reactions. All patients were able to consistently identify the foods that triggered their reactions. However, when the foods were administered blindly through a tube directly into the stomach, the only four individuals who had any symptoms were the four who had convincing histories of anaphylaxis. Five of the nineteen nonresponders walked out of the study when it became obvious that they were not reproducing their allergic symptoms with the food they claimed to be allergic to.

The placebo effect is another important factor that can complicate any medical study. A **placebo** is the so-called "sugar pill" or "dummy pill" that contains no active ingredient, whether it be medication or food substance. Its purpose in a challenge test or medical study is to measure the person's response to what he or she *believes* to be the real food or medication. Placebos can cause many different symptoms, such as cough, headache, itching, wheezing, and high blood pressure. There are studies showing that people can be addicted to placebos. The placebo effect has been shown to be 35 percent, which is higher than many medicines on the market! Therefore, any scientifically sound study has to account for the placebo effect by using a control group of patients who are given placebo in a "blinded" fashion so they do not know whether they are being given the study food or a placebo. The food or placebo is given in a capsule that is tasteless, giving no clue to its contents. The code telling what each capsule contains is sealed until the end of the study. Once the study with both food and placebo capsules is completed, the seal on the code is broken, and the results can be tabulated. If the person's symptoms are reproduced with the food and not with the placebo, using the DBPCFC method, the diagnosis of the food-specific allergy can be made.

The danger of any challenge method is the possibility of inducing anaphylaxis in the allergic individual. Obviously, challenges should be done only in a medical facility capable of treating anaphylaxis. If the actual amount of food that caused the reaction is known, graded smaller concentrations of the food can be used sequentially in the challenge procedure, building up to the actual amount that was originally ingested. This approach increases the safety of the procedure. From a scientific point of view, the DBPCFC is considered the "gold standard" for the diagnosis of food allergy. Although the DBPCFC can be performed in your allergist's office, it is usually performed in a hospital setting.

For most cases of peanut allergy, the history of an immediate reaction to ingestion or contact with peanut, confirmed with a positive skin prick test or RAST test, is sufficient for diagnosis; a peanut challenge is seldom necessary to diagnose peanut allergy. In my practice, I usually order peanut challenges to determine whether a patient has outgrown or resolved peanut allergy.

**What is the youngest age for a food challenge?**

The purpose of a food challenge is to see whether the suspect food will cause actual symptoms when ingested. At the first sign of a reaction, either observed by the patient or by the doctor and nurse supervising the challenge, the procedure is stopped. The initial reactions many patients experience during challenges are often very subtle, such as mild discomfort in the throat, mouth, or lips. We rely on the patient to communicate these symptoms during the challenge to know when to stop the challenge. By the time the doctor or nurse actually observes symptoms such as hives, swelling, or difficulty breathing, the reaction has already progressed to a more severe level and the patient might already be uncomfortable and require medications to reverse the reaction.

A very young child is often incapable of communicating these symptoms, as are mentally challenged patients and patients with communicative disorders. I generally consider doing food challenges only on people with the required degree of ability to communicate. For children, I start using food challenges at age 4 or 5, depending on the given child's level of communication and understanding of the procedure.

### What is an elimination diet?

Andrew is three years old and has had severe eczema since age six months. He was evaluated in my office last month, and skin tests showed allergies to milk and eggs. I recommended eliminating all milk and egg products from his diet. On his follow-up appointment, he still had significant eczema, although it was less extensive than it was before his diet. I learned on close questioning that, when at his grandmother's house, he was still eating some baked goods that contained milk and eggs. Once this was eliminated, Andrew's eczema was much easier to control.

---

When you suspect food allergies but are not entirely certain which foods are the cause, an elimination diet can be the answer. Such a diet completely and strictly eliminates each suspect food for a certain time period. It starts with the original list of suspect foods, from a careful analysis of your food and symptom diary and your medical history. If the symptoms persist despite a careful elimination diet, screening allergy tests such as skin prick tests or IgE RAST tests might help narrow down the list or screen for foods that were not originally suspected.

Once you make a list of suspect foods, you and your physician can design an elimination diet. The diet has to be completely free from the suspect foods, including products containing and cooked with the foods, and all possible hidden sources of the foods. The greater the number of foods to be eliminated, the more difficult the elimination. Ideally, the elimination period should be two weeks. If your symptoms resolve during that period of elimination, you have found a possible cause. If the symptoms persist despite the elimination diet, it is unlikely that the suspect foods were relevant, and you might then proceed to other possible foods. An elimination diet should only be done under a physician's supervision to avoid the possibility of any nutritional deficiencies.

### Elemental Diets

If the elimination diet to select foods did not resolve symptoms, the next step is to go on an elemental diet. Elemental diets are essentially allergen-free formulas that are nutritionally complete in proteins, fats, and carbohydrates. Examples of elemental infant formulas are Neocate and Elecare. Pregestimil, Alimentum, and Nutramigen are hypoallergenic formulas that contain small protein fragments or peptides. For adults, Vivonex is available as well. An elemental diet is a rather extreme alternative, but if it fails to resolve your symptoms, you can be reasonably sure that you don't have a food allergy.

If the symptoms do resolve when you are on an elemental diet, the next step is to reproduce the symptoms by direct challenge. This is ideally done by DBPCFC, but an open challenge can be considered if the skin or RAST test is negative and the actual history is rather doubtful for allergy. In this situation, the risk for anaphylaxis is low and the challenge is fairly safe to perform in the office. Food challenges should never be done at home if there is even a remote chance that anaphylaxis or severe symptoms could occur.

The confirmed diagnosis of a food allergy is made when the elimination of the offending food resolves the symptoms and when challenge with the offending food reproduces the symptoms.

### Are there food reactions that aren't allergies?

Reactions to foods can occur by mechanisms other than allergic reactions. Food intolerance can occur in individuals whose digestive systems are unable to digest and metabolize food, resulting in undigested or partially digested food, which can then lead to bacterial overgrowth, diarrhea, gas formation, and abdominal pain and cramping. Lactose intolerance is probably the most common example, occurring in 5 percent of the Caucasian population but in as much as 60 to 90 percent of Blacks, Hispanics, and Asians. Because people with lactose intolerance are unable to digest lactose, the major sugar in milk, they often mistakenly believe that their intolerance of milk is a milk allergy. Although milk avoidance is the treatment plan for patients with lactose intolerance just as it is for milk-allergic patients, the mechanisms for their respective problems are very different.

Because skin testing and RAST testing will only detect allergen-specific IgE, these tests will not help diagnose food intolerances or other types of adverse food reactions in which IgE is not involved. Skin tests and RAST tests performed on these individuals will be negative. Most children with milk allergies will outgrow the problem. Most people with lactose intolerance have it as a permanent condition. Many, however, are able to tolerate varying amounts of dairy products in their diet, depending on the severity of their condition.

Another example of a non-IgE mediated food problem is celiac disease, in which gluten, a protein found in wheat, rye, and barley, triggers an inflammatory reaction in the small intestine. It results in symptoms of abdominal pain, bloating, diarrhea, and weight loss caused by failure of the small intestine to absorb nutrients. Patients with this disease need to avoid wheat, rye, barley, and other gluten-containing foods and additives. Remember, because lactose intolerance and celiac disease are not allergic disorders, allergy testing for the milk and wheat proteins will be negative. These disorders affect the digestive tract, so they carry no risk of respiratory symptoms or anaphylaxis.

# CHAPTER 2

# PEANUT ALLERGY 101

**What is the historical background of peanut allergy?**
Peanuts are thought to have originated in eastern Bolivia and were cultivated for food at least as early as 2,000 or 3,000 BCE. The ancient Peruvians considered peanuts so important that they buried their dead with pots of peanuts to accompany them to the afterlife. The Spanish explorers of the fifteenth century brought the peanut back to Europe and then to the Philippines and Indonesia. It spread to Vietnam and China by the 1700s and subsequently from China to Japan. The Portuguese brought the peanut to Africa in the 1500s, which then later spread to India. The English and French were cultivating peanuts by the 1700s.

The American biochemist George Washington Carver (1860–1943) is given credit for developing the many modern uses of peanuts. He was interested in enriching the nutrition of minorities and the poor, and peanuts provide a highly nutritious and inexpensive source of easily digestible protein. Peanuts also are an excellent source of vitamin B12 (niacin), vitamin E, magnesium, chromium, and manganese. These nutrients are typically found in meats, whole grains, legumes, and vegetable oils. The peanut's versatility and ability to be prepared in so many forms—eaten whole as a vegetable, roasted and salted as a snack, crushed and ground as a spread or "butter," and incorporated into candy, baked goods, and other foods—was ideal for Dr. Carver. It could also be used for cooking oil, which was extracted by pressure or solvents. Dr. Carver discovered more than 300 uses for the peanut, including the manufacturing of plastics, adhesives, bleaches, and linoleum, among others.

The cultivation of peanuts and the manufacturing of peanut products became important sources of employment and remain so to the present. The U.S., particularly the southern states, remains one of the world's largest producers of peanuts, along with China and India. Seven states account for approximately 98 percent of all peanuts grown in the U.S. Georgia (38 percent) accounts for the major production of peanuts, followed by Texas (23 percent), Alabama (10 percent), North Carolina (9 percent), Florida (6 percent), Virginia (5 percent), and Oklahoma (5 percent). There are about 40,000 peanut farms in these peanut-producing regions. The contribution of peanuts to the U.S. economy is $4 billion a year. Annual peanut consumption in the U.S. is nearly 1.7 billion pounds, or about 11 pounds per person, of which more than half is in the form of peanut butter.

Peanut butter was invented in the 1800s and popularized by John Harvey Kellogg, who invented corn flakes. The first recipe for the peanut butter and jelly sandwich was published in 1901, and by the Depression era, the peanut butter sandwich was one of the most popular food items for children in the U.S. Peanut butter has been a staple of the American diet ever since and is found in 75 percent of households.

### The History of Peanut Allergy in Medicine

As early as the fourth century BCE, Hippocrates observed that milk could induce hives and gastric upset. Food allergy was first recognized as a clinical entity in 1921 by Prausnitz and Kustner. The first definite reference to nut allergy in medical literature was in 1920 by the noted hematologist Dr. Kenneth Blackfan. He observed a ten-year-old child, whose eczema was "always intensified" by nuts, eggs, and fish. "The eating of any of them was followed almost immediately by a burning sensation in the throat, vomiting, diarrhea, edema of the lips and ears and urticaria."

There was no research in the field of peanut allergy until as recently as 1978, when Bock reported on fourteen children with peanut allergy, proven by direct challenge. In 1981, Taylor reported ten patients with peanut allergy who ingested encapsulated peanut oil without any allergic reactions, suggesting that peanut oil was not allergenic. In 1984, Sampson and Albergo showed that positive skin prick tests and RAST tests to peanut correlate 100 percent with positive challenge to peanut, establishing the usefulness of these allergy tests in the diagnosis of peanut allergy.

In 1988, Yunginger reported fatal anaphylaxis to food in seven patients, four of whom turned out to have peanut allergy. In 1992, Sampson reported thirteen patients with fatal and near-fatal food anaphylaxis, seven of whom had peanut allergy. Of the six patients with fatal anaphylaxis, four were allergic to peanuts. Both reports emphasized the great risk in delaying the administration of epinephrine to patients experiencing anaphylaxis. In 1989, Bock and Atkins showed that peanut allergy in childhood usually persists into adulthood. In 1992, Leung and his colleagues reported three patients with peanut anaphylaxis successfully treated with immunotherapy to peanut extract. However, the rate of systemic reactions to the therapy was very high at 13 percent.

In 2003, Leung, Sampson, and colleagues reported on the successful use of an anti-IgE vaccine in preventing anaphylaxis in peanut-allergic patients. By blocking all IgE in the body, this vaccine decreases all allergic reactions caused by IgE such as peanut allergy. Patients who previously could only tolerate half a peanut before reacting could subsequently tolerate up to nine peanuts after the vaccinations. Recent studies now show that 20 percent of peanut-allergic patients can outgrow their allergy by the age of six.

Much current research has focused on the immunology and molecular biology of peanut allergy, characterizing the specific proteins causing IgE-mediated reactions. This research has led to successful gene sequencing and cloning of peanut protein. Using this information, several laboratories are working on potential vaccines for peanut allergy and other potential techniques for treatment, and biotechnology laboratories in the food industry are working on a nonallergenic peanut. If you are interested in learning more about the studies mentioned in this chapter or throughout the rest of the book, please see Appendix D.

### How common is peanut allergy?

Current estimates show that approximately 1.2 to 1.5 percent of children in the U.S., Canada and the U.K., and up to 3 million Americans are affected by peanut allergy. Dr. Scott Sicherer's (of Mount Sinai School of Medicine in New York) 1999 telephone survey study showed a 1.1 percent prevalence of peanut and nut allergy in the U.S., or approximately 3 million Americans, including both children and adults. The prevalence of peanut allergy alone is 0.6 percent of the population. A five-year follow-up study published by Dr. Sicherer in 2003 showed a similar overall prevalence rate in adults, but it showed a doubling in the prevalence rate in children, from 0.6 percent to 1.2 percent. A British study showed that one in 200 four year olds have peanut allergy. One percent of all British preschool students are estimated to be affected. Infants and toddlers are particularly susceptible to peanut allergy; a recent study showed that peanut-allergic patients had their first allergic reaction at an average age of 22 months. A 2003 Canadian study of 4,339 school children showed a 1.5 percent prevalence of peanut allergy, confirmed by allergy testing. A study of eighty-one children with a history of food allergies by May and Bock showed that 21 percent of these patients had peanut allergy by double-blind food challenges. Comparing peanut allergy to other food allergies, 2.5

percent of newborn infants are allergic to cow's milk in the first year of life, and 15 percent retain this allergy into their second decade of life. Egg allergy occurs in 1.3 percent of children. Shellfish allergy occurs in approximately 0.5 percent of the population. Peanuts are by far the most common cause of food anaphylaxis.

### Frequency of Food Allergies in Children and Adults

| Food | Children | Adults |
|------|----------|--------|
| Milk | 2.5% | n/a |
| Egg | 1.3% | n/a |
| Peanut | 0.8% | 0.6% |
| Wheat | 0.4% | n/a |
| Soy | 0.4% | n/a |
| Tree nuts | 0.2% | 0.5% |
| Fish | 0.1% | 0.4% |
| Shellfish | 0.1% | 2.0% |

Another study found that, of 185 infants, 80 percent had been exposed to peanut products by the age of one year, and 100 percent had exposure by age two. Follow up at age seven showed that 7 percent of high-risk children tested positive to peanut, and 4 percent had definite reactions to peanut by history or actual challenge. Dr. Hugh Sampson has observed a doubling in the number of peanut-allergic children over the past five years, and the number of allergic reactions to peanuts in both children and adults has increased by 95 percent over the same time span. This increased prevalence of peanut allergy is consistent with the reports of allergists across the country and worldwide.

## Why has peanut allergy increased so dramatically, particularly in young children?

The answer to this question is complex. There has certainly been an increase in all allergic diseases in young children, with a doubling in the numbers of children with asthma, environmental allergies, eczema, and all food allergies, such as those to milk and eggs. The increase in peanut allergy probably parallels this general increase in all allergic diseases in children. The question that naturally follows is, "Why are all of these allergic conditions so common in young children now, compared to less than one generation ago?" There have been numerous theories to explain this increase. The theory that seems to have the most support from laboratory and clinical studies is the "Hygiene Hypothesis."

## What is the Hygiene Hypothesis?

One of the initial studies leading to the Hygiene Hypothesis was the observation that, before the Berlin Wall came down, East German children had much lower rates of asthma than did West German children, despite higher rates of air pollution, more tobacco smoking, lower rates of childhood immunizations, poorer socioeconomic status, and poorer public health conditions. The more "hygienic" society seemed more allergic!

Another interesting study from the University of Arizona compared asthma rates in children who grew up in daycare where respiratory illnesses, coughing, and wheezing were often the norm, versus children who grew up in more sheltered environments and did not experience frequent respiratory illnesses. The asthma rates were surprisingly higher in children who did not grow up in daycare conditions, again showing that a more hygienic infancy period predisposed children to a more allergic outcome later in childhood.

Subsequent laboratory studies in animals and humans suggest that the immune system in early infancy is primed to recognize and fight infections. In the absence of infections, the immune system is "re-set" to target innocuous items in the child's diet and environment, resulting in abnormal reactions to harmless things such as food, pets, pollens, and dust mites. The exposures in the first few years of life seem to be critical in determining whether the child develops allergies and asthma.

Some studies in Europe are now underway, examining the possible use of "probiotics," so-called good bacteria, in pregnancy and infancy as a way of turning off the "Hygiene Hypothesis switch." I am sure that this very active area of research will yield very interesting and useful findings in the near future.

### Why is peanut allergy more common in the U.S., U.K., and Australia than in Europe, Asia, and the Middle East?

In the U.S., peanut allergy is the third most common food allergy in children behind milk and egg allergy. In Israel, sesame allergy is third, behind milk and egg allergy, ahead of peanut allergy. This difference most likely reflects the differences in dietary practices. In the Middle East, sesame products and sesame paste are more commonly used than peanut butter.

In China, the world's leader in peanut production, peanut consumption is comparable to that this country, but peanut allergy is much less common. The explanation for this may be that peanuts in the Chinese diet are usually boiled or fried, as opposed to the peanut butter and dry-roasted peanuts in the Western diet. Laboratory studies show that the higher processing temperatures used in manufacturing peanut butter and dry-roasted peanuts result in an increase in the allergenicity of the peanut proteins. The lower cooking temperatures used in boiling or frying peanuts do not cause this increase, so boiled and fried peanuts are relatively less allergenic than dry-roasted peanuts or peanut butter.

### Is peanut allergy hereditary?

Peter is a thirty-one-year-old man with lifelong history of peanut and tree nut allergy. His mother and sister have food allergies, but not to peanut. His wife has hay fever, but no food allergies. She is pregnant with their first child, and they would like to know their baby's chances of developing peanut allergy.

---

It is well known that allergic diseases such as asthma, hay fever, and eczema cluster in families, and the individual often inherits one or more of the allergic diseases together. Food allergy is inherited, but whether allergies to specific foods such as peanut are inherited has not been extensively studied. Dr. Jonathan O'B. Hourihane, a prominent British peanut allergy researcher from University of Southampton, examined fifty peanut-allergic children and their forty-nine mothers, forty-eight fathers, and forty-five siblings with questionnaires and skin prick tests. This study showed that all types of allergic diseases become more common in successive generations and occur more often in maternal relatives than in paternal relatives. Thus, you are more likely to suffer from peanut allergy if one of your siblings has it than if one of your parents has it.

The study showed that not only is peanut allergy inherited but the tendency for all the other allergic diseases is inherited as well. Most recently, a study by Dr. Scott Sicherer and his colleagues at Mount Sinai School of Medicine in New York examined seventy-four identical and fraternal twin pairs in which at least one twin had peanut allergy. The pairs were recruited from the Food Allergy & Anaphylaxis Network. Among identical twins, both twins were peanut-allergic in 64 percent, whereas in fraternal twins, the concordance rate was 7 percent, which is the same as the concordance rate observed in non-twin siblings. These results strongly indicate that there is significant genetic influence on peanut allergy.

Although I am not routinely recommending that all symptom-free siblings of a peanut-allergic child be tested for peanut allergy, I feel that such testing is reasonable if the family requests it for their own reassurance. More studies have to be performed before a general policy on testing siblings is universally accepted.

### How early can peanut sensitization occur?

Caitlin's mother first suspected that Caitlin was allergic to peanuts when each time after eating peanuts or peanut butter herself and then breast feeding Caitlin, the baby became very irritable. When Caitlin was four weeks old, she developed an itchy red rash on her face, which also flared up after breast feeding. At that point, her mother stopped eating peanut products. Caitlin was weaned completely from breast milk by six-months of age. She was kept away from all peanut products until she was two years old. The very first time she was given peanut butter on a cracker, she developed hives all over her body and started wheezing. She was referred to me by the emergency room physician who treated her for that reaction.

---

Sensitization to peanut can occur very early in life, perhaps due to the high potency of the peanut allergens. One study showed that 80 percent of peanut-allergic individuals developed allergic symptoms on their first known exposure. A French study of newborn infants younger than eleven days and babies between age seventeen days and four months showed that 8 percent had positive skin tests to peanut. This certainly implies that sensitization occurred either shortly after birth or in the womb.

One very interesting study by Hourihane from the U.K. showed a correlation between the self-reported increased consumption of peanuts by pregnant and nursing mothers and a definite decrease in the age of onset of peanut allergy over the past ten years. In other words, the more peanut products consumed by pregnant and nursing mothers, the younger the age at which their children developed their peanut allergies. Studies show that the fetus is capable of being sensitized to milk protein; although the studies on peanut have not yet been done, peanut protein is such a potent allergen that it is more than likely capable of doing the same. Therefore, a pregnant mother's diet can affect her child's likelihood of developing food allergies.

---

### Eating Peanuts While Breast Feeding

Peanut proteins can be detected in breast milk for several hours after the mother has eaten peanuts. What this means is that an exclusively breast fed baby can still be exposed to peanut protein and become sensitized to peanut through the mother. Babies with peanut allergies can develop allergic symptoms following nursing if the mother has recently eaten peanuts. Because a family history of allergic disorders such as hay fever, asthma, and eczema is a risk factor for the development of food allergy, it may be prudent for the pregnant and nursing woman with this type of family history to avoid such allergenic foods.

---

Another potential route of sensitization is peanut-oil-based vitamin preparations and infant formulas. These items are a problem primarily in Europe and are mentioned here to alert the traveler who might unknowingly make purchases of products that in the U.S. normally would not contain peanut oil.

A report from France studied 122 children ages seven months to five years old. During the first two years of life, one group of children received vitamin D free from peanut oil, and two groups received vitamin D containing peanut oil. The two groups receiving vitamin D containing peanut oil had positive skin tests to peanut, while the group receiving peanut-oil-free vitamin D had significantly less sensitization on skin testing. Most American brands of vitamins, such as Flintstones Supplements, One-A-Day, and Bugs Bunny Vitamins, do not contain peanut oil.

There is a report on the presence of allergenic peanut oil in milk formula in the British medical journal *Lancet* from 1991, but to my knowledge, no American infant formulas contain peanut oil.

Always be extra cautious when traveling abroad because of different practices in foreign countries. Topical creams and lotions can also contain peanut oils. Children with damaged skin due to chronic inflammatory skin conditions, such as eczema, are probably most susceptible to sensitization from topical preparations. Most pharmaceutical-grade peanut oils contain no detectable levels of peanut protein, but it is certainly possible that the low levels of peanut protein that can cause sensitization are too low to be detectable by available technology.

### What in peanuts make them so allergenic?

John is a twenty-five-year-old man with a lifelong history of peanut and tree nut allergies, as well as egg, wheat, and soy allergies. He had an anaphylactic reaction at age thirteen when he accidentally was given some brownies that had nuts in them. He has been extremely careful about avoiding all nuts since then without any further problems. He has had mild hives with egg, wheat, and soy products, but never anaphylaxis.

---

The answer lies in the part of the peanut that actually causes the allergy: the peanut proteins. Allergic reactions result from our body's immune responses to proteins. In milk, the milk proteins are casein and the major whey proteins, lactalbumin and lactoglobulin. In egg white, they are ovalbumin and ovomucoid. In wheat, it is gluten, and in shrimp, it is tropomyosin.

The allergenic peanut proteins are the seed-storage proteins vicilin, conglutin, and glycinin. By understanding the nature of these peanut proteins, scientists are beginning to unlock the mystery of why peanuts are among the most potent of all food allergens. The protein content of a peanut is 24.3 percent of the average weight of a peanut. The allergenic proteins in peanuts are found in the cotyledon, or embryonic leaf, of the peanut seed plant. These proteins, like other food allergens, are glycoproteins, which are proteins that have sugars as part of their structure.

Work from several laboratories has identified three major allergenic proteins from peanuts, called Ara h1, Ara h2, and Ara h3. Ara is derived from arachia, the Latin term for peanut. The genes for these allergens have been cloned and sequenced. Ara h1 belongs to the vicilin family of seed-storage proteins, Ara h2 belongs to the conglutin family, and the most recently identified peanut allergen, Ara h3, belongs to the glycinin family. Ninety five percent of peanut-allergic patients react to Ara h1 and Ara h2, while approximately 50 percent of peanut-allergic patients react to Ara h3. Ara h2 is the most potent allergenic protein of the three. Four additional minor proteins have been identified: Ara h5, Ara h6, Ara h7 and Ara h8. These minor proteins are less important as peanut-allergic patients react to them less than 50 percent of the time.

Scientists have discovered some structural features of Ara h1 called **epitopes,** and how this feature binds to IgE could explain why it is such an extremely allergenic protein. With this information, researchers are now working on ways to alter the structure of this protein and hope that a "hypoallergenic peanut" might be created that retained all of characteristics of a peanut. There is also research being conducted to create vaccines to these peanut allergens.

### Is the peanut a true nut?

Peanuts are vegetables; nuts are fruits. Peanuts (botanical name *Arachia hypogea*) are actually members of the legume family, which includes lentils, soybeans, peas, black-eyed peas, chickpeas, lima beans, kidney beans, green beans, and garbanzo beans. Peanuts are native to South America, and several varieties are grown in the U.S. These include the Virginia, Spanish, and runner variety.

Unlike tree nuts, which grow on trees, peanuts grow in the ground. The peanut plant is a bushy, flowering annual. After fertilization, the flower stalk elongates until its weight causes it to bend down and touch the ground. Continued growth of the stalk pushes the ovary into the ground, and the seeds grow, forming the familiar peanuts.

The botanical definition of a true nut is a hard, dry, closed, one-seeded fruit. In general, the term nut can apply to any seed or dried fruit of a woody plant that does not belong to the legume family. The tree nuts commonly eaten and capable of causing allergies are walnuts, almonds, cashews, pecans, Brazil nuts, hazelnuts, Macadamia nuts, and pistachios.

Almonds, pecans, and pistachios are the seeds of fruits. The fruit contains a pit that encloses the nut. Almonds come in two types: Sweet almond, which is the edible kind, and bitter almond, which is poisonous (although the oil can be extracted and is safe to use). Walnuts come in three varieties: black, English, and Persian walnuts. Pecans are related to hickory nuts and are covered by a leathery skin. Brazil nuts are the seed of large woody fruits. They include creamnut, chestnut of Para, and sapucaia or paradise nut. The cashew nut is the seed of a pearlike fruit that must be roasted to be palatable. The pistachio, sometimes known as the green almond, is also the seed of a drupe, like the almond and pecan. Piñon, or pine nuts, are the seeds of pines and are found in pine cones. Pignolia nuts are the seeds of the European pine and resemble pine nuts. The hazelnut, or filbert, is a true nut and is the seed of a pearlike green fruit. Other true nuts are acorns and beechnuts, which are primarily used for animal feed, and chestnuts. Macadamia nuts are also called Queensland, Australian Gympie, Bush, and Bopple nuts. The seed is contained in a fruit with a fleshy husk, and the thin shell of the seed is cracked to release the nut.

Although many people are allergic to more than one nut, some people have just one solitary tree nut allergy.

### Are there nuts that do not commonly cause allergies?

The coconut is also the seed of a fruit, but it is generally not restricted from the diet of tree-nut-allergic people. Other non-allergenic nuts found in other parts of the world are ginkgo nuts used in Chinese and Asian cooking, Pili or Javanese almonds, terminalia, wingnuts, and Kola nuts. Water chestnuts, nutmeg, and mace are not nuts and do not need to be avoided by tree-nut-allergic people. Shea nut butter is from the fruit of the Karite tree of Ghana, *butyrosperum parkii*. It is not actually from a nut but instead is derived from pressing the whole fruit, which is much like an avocado. The slightly greenish butter from the shea nut has soothing protecting qualities and sunscreening properties, and it can be found in many creams, lotions, and cosmetics. It does not need to be avoided by nut-allergic individuals.

### Should all members of a food family be avoided if you are allergic to one food in that family?

Anne is thirty-six and recently married a Greek man who brings her to visit his family in Athens every summer. She has developed allergy symptoms to some Greek dishes and has experienced hives, diarrhea, and, on one occasion, wheezing. She thinks she is allergic to some of the spices such as parsley, dill, caraway, and anise. Her food skin tests were positive to celery and carrots, both members of the Umbelliferae family to which parsley, dill, caraway, anise, coriander, and fennel also belong. She tries to avoid all members of this food family but has trouble convincing her Greek mother-in-law of her allergy problem.

The prevailing thought at one time was that being allergic to one type of legume meant that you would cross-react to all members of the legume family regardless of previous exposure or history. Because peanuts are legumes, people allergic to peanuts were therefore advised to avoid not only peanuts but all members of the legume family, regardless of whether they had ever had a reaction to other legumes. To take this logic further, it was also a common belief that being allergic to one member of a food group automatically made you allergic to every food in that group. This theory was based on the work by Vaughan and Black in 1929, when they classified foods into botanically related food groups. They concluded that cross-reactions would occur between foods belonging to the same food family similar to the cross-reactions observed in pollen allergies.

Recent studies by Bock and others at the National Jewish Medical and Research Center in Denver, Colorado, show that this type of cross-reactivity does not commonly occur. Sampson of the Jaffe Food Allergy Institute in New York studied sixty-nine patients with one or more positive skin tests to legumes and gave them oral double-blind placebo-controlled food challenges in the hospital with five legumes: peanut, soybean, pea, green bean, and lima bean. Only two patients had a positive food challenge to more than one legume. They concluded that clinically relevant cross-reactivity to legumes is very rare and that clinical sensitivity to one legume does not warrant dietary elimination of the entire legume food family unless sensitivity to each food is confirmed by blind oral challenges.

There is one special consideration regarding other legumes. A recent report by Moneret-Vautrin from France demonstrated cross-reactivity between peanut and another legume, the lupines. The lupine is consumed either in the form of seeds or as flour used to supplement wheat flour. In France, up to 10 percent lupine flour can be added to wheat flour and is not subject to labeling. Lupine flour is used in baked goods, pasta, sauces, milk, and soy substitutes. There have been several reports of lupine allergy. This study examined twenty-four peanut-allergic individuals for lupine allergy and found positive skin prick tests in 44 percent. In six people challenged by DBPCFC, five were positive to lupine. The blood from four individuals demonstrated RAST inhibition to lupine by peanut, demonstrating cross-reactivity. The authors warn that cross-reactivity to this legume hidden in wheat flour can be a serious problem for the peanut-allergic individual. Read labels of imported foods, especially baked goods, for lupine or lupine flour, and avoid them.

You can be allergic to multiple foods, including foods in the same family, but this is usually a result of separate allergies, not a common cross-reacting allergy. In general, you need avoid only the specific food you are allergic to by history, and it is not necessary to avoid the entire food family. The two main exceptions to this recommendation would be the tree nuts and the crustacean shellfish (i.e., shrimp, lobster, crab). There does seem to be cross-reactivity among members of these food groups.

The rate of cross-reactivity between a tree nut with other tree nuts is greater than 50 percent. A recent study showed that walnut, pecan, and hazelnut constitute a group of cross-reactive nuts and belong to the same botanical sub-family. Cashew, pistachio, almond, and Brazil nut are another closely related subclass of cross-reactive nuts, and of these, cashew and pistachio strongly cross-react with each other. Peanuts cross react with tree nuts 35 percent of the time but with legumes less than 10 percent of the time. Soybeans react with other legumes less than 5 percent of the time. The rate of cross-reactivity of wheat with other grains is 25 percent. With animal proteins, beef and lamb cross-react 50 percent of the time, fish species cross-react with other fish species more than 50 percent of the time, and shellfish cross-react with other shellfish 50 to 75 percent of the time.

If you are allergic to peanuts, you should also avoid tree nuts, but it is safe to eat legumes. If you are allergic to one tree nut, avoid all other tree nuts.

### Are peanut-allergic individuals also allergic to tree nuts?

Investigators studying peanut-allergic individuals have found coexisting tree nut allergies in 34 percent to 50 percent of those people, depending on the study. Among patients with tree nut allergy, 22 percent reported having reactions to more than one tree nut. It is unknown whether the coexistence of peanut and tree nut allergies is due to cross-reacting proteins or whether this reflects a general increase in the tendency to react to highly allergenic proteins in an allergic individual. This may not necessarily be due to specific allergens, such as peanuts or tree nuts, but it may apply to all allergenic foods. This is supported by Sampson's study, which showed that of the peanut and tree-nut allergic population, 57 percent are also allergic to egg, 37 percent are also allergic to milk, and 29 percent are also allergic to fish and shellfish. People who are allergic to one food seem to have the tendency to be allergic to others. On the other hand, there is some evidence of cross-reactivity between peanuts, walnuts, and pecans.

### Should peanut-allergic individuals avoid tree nuts?

Clearly, there are many people with peanut allergy who can eat tree nuts with no problem and many people with tree-nut allergies who can eat peanuts. However, many allergists, myself included, recommend that children allergic to peanuts avoid all tree nuts. The rationale for this recommendation is the difficulty in identifying specific nuts, particularly in mixtures and in processed food; the significant potential for peanuts contaminating other nuts; and the recognition that tree-nut allergy is also potentially severe and lifelong.

### Should peanut- and nut-allergic individuals avoid seeds?

Sesame seed allergy is becoming common throughout the world, particularly in Middle Eastern countries such as Israel. Sesame seed allergy is more common than peanut allergy and is exceeded only by milk and egg allergy. This increase in sesame allergy most likely reflects the dietary practices of Middle Eastern countries, where sesame paste is an important food. The allergenic proteins in sesame seed share some similarities to Ara h1, the major peanut allergen. The risk of having sesame seed allergy in peanut- and nut-allergic patients hasn't been carefully studied, but it is thought to be low, about 5 to 10 percent. Because sesame seed allergy can be associated with anaphylaxis and sesame seed is a common food ingredient, I often include it when I test a patient for peanut and tree nuts. If the tests are positive, I recommend avoiding it.

### Does soy formula cause peanut allergy in infants?

This issue was raised by a 2003 study by Dr. Gideon Lack and his colleagues from London, England, which showed that in children with peanut allergy, consumption of soy formula was three to four times more common than in children with no history of peanut allergy. The children with peanut allergy were also more likely to have eczema and rashes and a history of exposure to skin creams containing peanut oil. There is some controversy about this study's conclusion of a relationship between soy formula and development of peanut allergy, as these infants clearly had food allergies and, for that reason alone, could have been placed on soy formula. The investigators stated that their analysis showed an independent correlation between soy consumption and peanut allergy, and they stated that the use of soy formula as a response to allergy and eczema could not explain their findings. They reasoned that some similarities in the proteins of soy and peanut could explain their results.

This issue of soy and peanut allergy was resolved with a 2005 Finnish study consisting of a double-blinded study of 170 infants ages eleven to two months with milk allergy. The infants were randomized to receive either a hypoallergenic infant formula or a soy protein-based formula for two years, and they were followed for four years. At the age of four years, there was no difference in the number of peanut-allergic children between the two groups. There was also no difference in sensitization to peanut measured by RAST testing between the two groups. The authors conclude that soy formula does not lead to the development of peanut allergy.

### Can peanut protein be found in breast milk?

Dr. Peter Vadas and his colleagues studied this question in twenty-three lactating women by feeding them dry-roasted peanuts and then measuring peanut protein in their expressed breast milk. There was measurable peanut protein in eleven of the women, with average peak levels occurring one hour after eating the peanuts. The peanut protein level had declined to negligible levels for nine women by four hours after, but two women had detectable levels at four hours and one woman had it for eight hours after eating peanuts. The amounts measured were very low but potentially enough to cause a reaction in a peanut-allergic infant and enough to cause sensitization in an allergy prone infant. I recommend that a nursing mother with a peanut-allergic infant restrict peanuts and peanut products from her diet.

### Can peanut allergy be transferred from person to person?

In 1997, a case report was published in the *New England Journal of Medicine* of a liver and kidney transplant recipient who developed a new peanut allergy. His donor organs apparently came from a man who had died from peanut anaphylaxis after eating satay sauce containing peanuts. The recipient had no prior history of peanut or food allergy. Three months after his transplant, the patient developed a skin rash and swelling of his throat after eating peanuts. The RAST test to peanuts was positive. Interestingly, a woman received a pancreas and the other kidney from the same peanut-allergic organ donor. She never developed peanut allergy, and she had a negative RAST to peanut. She was challenged with peanut and had no reaction.

The transfer of peanut allergy to the recipient most likely was the result of the transfer of white blood cells contained in the donor liver called B cells, which produce peanut-specific IgE. Similar transfer of peanut allergy with bone marrow transplantation has been reported. Because transplant recipients take drugs to suppress their normal immune response to allow survival of the donated organ, cells of the donor immune system are not destroyed by the recipient. This allows cells of the immune system, such as B cells secreting peanut-specific IgE contained in the liver and bone marrow, to survive, and these transplanted cells will perpetuate the peanut allergy in the transplant recipient.

In contrast, B cells and other cells of the immune system capable of causing allergies are not found in the pancreas or kidney, so these organ transplants do not transfer allergies from donor to recipient. Blood transfusions present no risk of transferring allergies because transfusion recipients are not immunosuppressed, and any donor B cells would be destroyed by the recipient's immune system. For organ recipients, the allergic B cells might eventually be destroyed as the patient's immunosuppressive drugs are tapered. For bone marrow recipients, the allergic B cells are an intrinsic part of the bone marrow, so there would never be any improvement in the transferred allergy.

Organ transplant recipients should be warned of the possibility of developing allergic reactions if their organ donor has a history of food allergy.

### Can organ transplantation cure peanut allergy?

Interestingly, just as peanut allergy can be transferred from an organ donor to an organ recipient as described above, there was a report in 2005 of a twelve-year-old peanut-allergic boy who, after receiving a bone marrow transplant for his immunodeficiency, completely resolved his peanut allergy. The bone marrow donor presumably was not allergic to peanut. This boy had had a lifelong history of eczema and allergies to peanut, pea, and lentil. At the time of his bone marrow transplant, he had outgrown his pea and lentil allergy, but his CAP RAST to peanut was still 23.1 kU/L and his total IgE level was 2,533 IU/L. He had a successful result from the bone marrow transplant with no more infections. Seventeen months after the transplant, his IgE had fallen to 40 IU/L and his CAP RAST to peanut was undetectable. Skin prick test to peanut was negative. He underwent an oral peanut challenge and was able to tolerate 8 grams of peanut. Since then, he has been consuming all peanut products with no problems.

By suppressing the boy's original immune system, his immune B cells causing peanut allergy were destroyed and then replaced by the immune cells of the non-peanut-allergic donor. The end result is that the boy now has the immune system of the bone marrow donor, with no peanut allergy. The investigators of this report conclude that, although their patient's peanut allergy was cured by bone marrow transplantation, such a drastic medical procedure is not a viable treatment for peanut allergy. This interesting case report gives much insight into the importance of the bone marrow cells in the mechanism of peanut allergy.

## Will I outgrow my peanut allergy?

Jason, age five, had peanut allergy diagnosed at age one when he developed hives from just touching his face with peanut butter. He was never exposed to peanut again and was strictly kept away from all peanut and nut products without any accidents and did well. His family never needed to use their EpiPen. He did not have any other allergy-related problems. When Jason was about to enter kindergarten, his mother wanted to know whether he was still allergic to peanuts. Skin tests to peanut and tree nuts were negative. He was challenged with peanut butter in the clinic and had no reaction. He can now eat everything without restrictions.

---

Most studies seem to indicate that peanut allergy, unlike allergies to milk, soy, egg, and wheat, are stable through time and not outgrown.

The first study to address the question of the natural history of food allergy was by S. Allan Bock of National Jewish Medical and Research Center in Denver, Colorado, in 1982. He studied eighty-seven children with proven food allergies. Fifty-six of the children were older than three years, and thirty-one children were younger than three years. Age three was chosen as a dividing point for the two study groups because all children older than age three, in the experience of the National Jewish Medical and Research Center, had IgE-mediated allergic reactions. The study was conducted with telephone interviews and follow-up DBPCFC. The elapsed time from initial testing to the follow-up interview ranged from several months to seven years.

In children older than three years, 19 percent of previously positive food challenges had turned negative at the time of follow-up. The most common foods to become tolerated with age were milk, egg, and soy. Peanut and tree nuts did not improve significantly. In children less than age three, 44 percent of the positive food challenges turned negative. Milk, egg, and soy again were the foods that were tolerated with age. Bock concluded that older children diagnosed with food allergy tended to not outgrow their food allergies, in contrast to younger children who were more likely to do so, especially those with milk and egg allergies. In several other studies, older children and adults have been shown to outgrow or lose their food allergies if they are able to completely eliminate the food allergen from their diet. The exceptions are the highly allergenic foods such as peanuts, tree nuts, fish, and shellfish.

To address the specific issue of whether peanut allergy is outgrown, Dr. Bock with Dr. Fred Atkins published in 1989, a follow-up study on thirty-two peanut-allergic children aged two years to fourteen years. These thirty-two patients all had impressive histories of peanut-allergic reactions, positive skin prick tests, and positive DBPCFC. Two to thirteen years after their initial evaluations, patients were contacted by telephone and gave updated information on the status of their peanut avoidance measures, their most recent peanut ingestion (both accidental and intentional), resultant symptoms and treatment required, and any subsequent allergy evaluation testing that had been done. All patients interviewed declined requests for repeat DBPCFC. Eight patients had successfully avoided any peanut ingestion. Seven patients had follow-up skin prick tests to peanut, and all remained positive from two to ten years after initial evaluation. Twenty-four patients out of the thirty-two had accidental ingestions; all ingestions resulted in symptoms, ranging from skin reactions (i.e., hives, swelling, eczema) to gastrointestinal to nasal and eye symptoms to wheezing, coughing, and laryngeal edema. No patient had a drop in blood pressure or anaphylaxis. The conclusion of the study is that peanut allergy is long lasting and does not appear to improve with time.

In 1998, Dr. Hourihane and his colleagues in the U.K. studied 120 children ages two years to ten years. They all had a convincing history of peanut allergy and all underwent open peanut challenge. Twenty-two children were identified who had outgrown peanut allergy, documented with negative challenges. Fifteen of these "resolvers" were matched by age with fifteen "persisters," and features of their history and symptoms were compared, as well as skin test and serum IgE results. The age of the first reaction to peanut, serum IgE, severity of reactions, and number of reactions were similar in both groups. There were no cases of anaphylaxis in this study. The time interval between the last reaction and challenge was longer, but not significantly so, in resolvers than in persisters. The resolvers also had negative skin test results or smaller results than persisters. The resolvers tended to have fewer food allergies.

Hourihane concluded that some preschool children with mild to moderate allergic reactions to peanuts have a 22/120, or 18 percent, chance of resolving or outgrowing the allergy. Follow-up of fourteen resolvers showed no reactions to peanuts on further peanut exposure. This study is consistent with my own clinical experience and that of others, which has shown that young children age two to three years who become allergic to peanuts only with mild, non-anaphylactic symptoms can outgrow their peanut allergy.

There have subsequently been several other studies all confirming that, for a subset of patients, peanut allergy can be outgrown. Vander Leek, et al. (2000) had a resolution rate of 23.5 percent in seventeen children. Spergel, et al. (2000) showed a resolution rate of 42 percent in thirty-three children. Skolnick, et al. (2001) showed a resolution rate of 21.5 percent in eighty-five children. Rangaraj et al. (2004) found 14 percent of twenty-nine children outgrew peanut allergy.

In my practice, the numbers of patients who outgrow peanut allergy are approximately 20 percent, comparable to the range found in these studies. The children who become successful resolvers also all had meticulous peanut and peanut product avoidance, with no accidental ingestions. Sampson has recommended that children who had an isolated peanut reaction in the first two years of life, and who have successfully avoided any further peanut reactions for three years or more, be retested by the CAP RAST and, if the result is low, to have skin prick testing done. Depending on the initial reaction history, a challenge can ultimately be performed to document the resolution or persistence of peanut allergy.

In contrast to the young children with peanut allergy, other studies, including Bock's, show that when peanut allergy develops in the older child or adult, it does not resolve with time.

In summary, approximately 20 percent of children outgrow or resolve their peanut allergy. These "resolvers" all have meticulous avoidance of peanut with nearly no accidental ingestions, smaller skin test results, and fewer food allergies in total. It is possible that the younger your child is when diagnosed with peanut allergy, the better his or her chances are of outgrowing it. I generally test young children with peanut allergy annually with CAP RAST tests to look for a trend in the levels. If they show a consistent downward trend, that child could potentially outgrow peanut allergy.

## When should my child have a peanut challenge to see whether the allergy has resolved?

Dr. David Fleischer and his colleagues at Johns Hopkins University and the University of Arkansas examined this question by doing peanut challenges on eighty peanut-allergic children with CAP RAST levels of 5 kU/L and lower, regardless of their history. Fifty-five percent of these patients passed the challenge. When the investigators analyzed the results further, they found that for patients with CAP RAST levels of 2 kU/L or less, 63 percent passed, and if their CAP RAST levels were less than 0.35 kU/L, 73 percent passed. Skin testing was not assessed in these patients during this study.

Children with levels of 2 kU/L or less were significantly more likely to pass the peanut challenge than children with levels between 2 and 5 kU/L. The authors of this study conclude that for children age 4 or older with CAP RAST levels less than 2 kU/L, it is reasonable to offer a peanut challenge as the chances of passing are greater than 50 percent. For doctors like myself who are in office-based practices, I recommend doing challenges only for patients for whom I have a very high expectation of passing. In my office, I challenge children older than age four years who have CAP RAST levels less than 0.35 kU/L and negative skin tests. Ninety-eight percent of these patients in my practice have successfully passed challenges. For patients for whom there is a significant chance of having a reaction, I recommend that the challenge be performed in a hospital setting.

### Can a food challenge be wrong?

There actually is a false negative rate of 1 to 3 percent for food challenges. So, after a patient passes the food challenge, a normal serving of the food should be eaten under supervision just to make sure that there is absolutely no problem.

### Is there a chance that, after I outgrow peanut allergy, the peanut allergy may come back?

In Dr. Fleischer's study, as well as several other reports, approximately 8 percent of patients who had successfully passed peanut challenges subsequently developed allergic reactions when they ate peanuts. There was no helpful information in the patient's testing or past history that could predict who would have a relapse of peanut allergy. Interestingly, all the patients who relapsed had continued to avoid eating peanuts, while the patients who ate peanuts were much less likely to relapse. It seems that after resolving peanut allergy, the continued exposure to peanut in the diet confers tolerance to peanut, but this tolerance is not maintained in the absence of peanut in the diet. Therefore, after you or your child have passed the peanut challenge, I would recommend that you include peanut and peanut products in your diet perhaps weekly or several times a month. Because we still do not fully understand all the risk factors for who will relapse, I recommend continuing to have an EpiPen or Twinject just in case.

### Can allergies to tree nuts be outgrown?

Dr. Fleischer and his colleagues at Johns Hopkins University studied 278 patients three to twenty-one years old with allergies to tree nuts. Almost two-thirds of the reactions were moderate to severe, and reactions to cashew and walnut accounted for nearly two-thirds of the severe reactions. Oral challenges were offered to patients aged four years and older, who had CAP RAST levels of less than 10 kU/L that had no reactions to tree nuts in the past year. Of the 278 patients, 117 met the challenge criteria on the basis of clinical history and CAP RAST levels. Of these 117 patients, seventy-eight declined to be challenged. The patients who declined to be challenged had significantly higher CAP RAST levels, were more allergic to other foods including peanut, and were less likely to have outgrown other food allergies. Of the thirty-nine patients who underwent oral challenges to tree nuts, twenty-three passed. As with peanut allergy, the CAP RAST levels were helpful in predicting who would pass the challenges: 58 percent with levels of 5 kU/L or less, 63 percent with levels of 2 kU/L or less, and 75 percent with levels less than 0.35 kU/L passed.

Another conclusion of the study was that outgrowing peanut allergy was associated with outgrowing tree nut allergy. Having allergies to more than one or two different tree nuts decreases the chances of outgrowing tree nut allergies. Even though only 9 percent (23 of 278 patients in the study) of tree nut allergic patients outgrow their allergies, I do recommend repeating the CAP RAST levels to tree nuts annually for children and would consider challenges if the child is age four or older and has CAP RAST less than 2 kU/L. At present, the rate of recurrence of tree nut allergy after it has been outgrown is unknown.

# CHAPTER 3

# ANAPHYLAXIS

## What is anaphylaxis?

At the party, George made sure to ask whether the sugar cookie he ate contained nuts because he had a severe peanut and tree nut allergy. The hostess assured him that they did not—she baked them herself. As soon as he took a bite of the cookie, George knew something was wrong. He felt his lips, tongue, and throat instantly swell, and his entire body became intensely itchy. Within a few minutes, he felt chest pain and tightness, and he could not breathe. His face and body were bright red and covered with hives. He had the feeling he was going to die. He was able to reach for his EpiPen and inject himself in the thigh before passing out. Luckily, his wife had already called 911, and by the time the paramedics arrived fifteen minutes later, George had regained consciousness and could breathe. He received another dose of epinephrine and was transported to the local hospital, where intravenous fluids, antihistamines, steroids, and aerosol asthma medications were given over the next twelve hours. He made a full recovery and was able to be discharged the following morning, completely back to normal. Later, the hostess of the party admitted that she had forgotten she had made the sugar cookies in the same mixing bowl that she had previously used to make cookies that contained nuts.

Anaphylaxis is the systemic manifestation of allergy—that is, it is when an allergic reaction affects the body as a whole and not just locally. In other words, some patients have hives just in the area of contact with the food allergen, such as the lips and mouth, while other patients erupt in hives over their entire body, regardless of the route of exposure. It is this latter systemic total body reaction that is termed anaphylaxis.

The severity of anaphylaxis can be graded mild, moderate, or severe. Dr. Simon Brown of Australia published a grading system for severity of anaphylaxis in 2004, based on the clinical features and symptoms of the reaction. The symptoms of mild anaphylaxis are hives, a sensation of fullness of the mouth and throat, swelling of the eyelids and lips, and nasal congestion. Moderate anaphylaxis would be accompanied by the additional symptoms of generalized or rapidly worsening hives and itching, swelling, flushing, tightness of the throat and chest, wheezing, and vomiting. The potential worse-case scenario is severe anaphylaxis, which is life-threatening. It can include severe swelling of the tissues of the upper airway, resulting in obstruction of breathing through the throat and blocking airflow in and out of the lungs. When the lower airways of the lungs narrow, shortness of breath, wheezing, and asthma can occur, compromising oxygenation.

When the cardiovascular system of the body undergoes anaphylaxis, massive tissue leakage from blood vessels results in decreased blood pressure and shock. Severe anaphylaxis is explosive in onset, usually occurring within minutes after exposure. Patients often have a "sense of impending doom" in the initial stages of severe anaphylaxis. Seizures can result from lack of oxygen. The combination of obstructed breathing and lack of oxygen with loss of heart function and blood pressure is often fatal.

The common causes of fatal anaphylaxis are bee stings, drug reactions, and food allergy. Annually in the U.S., there are 300 deaths from penicillin allergy, 150 deaths from food allergy, 90 percent of which are from peanuts and nuts, and fifty deaths from

## Grades of Anaphylaxis and Treatment

| Severity | Symptoms | Treatment |
|---|---|---|
| Mild | Skin involvement only | Antihistamines |
| Moderate | Generalized or rapidly progressive skin involvement, throat swelling, respiratory, gastrointestinal | Epinephrine, antihistamines, emergency medical attention |
| Severe | Cardiovascular shock, turning blue, loss of consciousness, death | Epinephrine, antihistamines, steroids, emergency medical attention, intensive care |

insect-sting anaphylaxis. By comparison, the annual death rate from asthma attacks is approximately 5,000. The majority of food anaphylaxis results from peanuts, tree nuts, and shellfish.

There are other conditions that can mimic the symptoms of anaphylaxis. Chest tightness and difficulty breathing can be a symptom of asthma, heartburn, or anxiety. A heart attack is sometimes very similar to an anaphylactic reaction, so prompt medical attention by a physician is crucial so that proper and appropriate treatment can be given.

## Is anaphylaxis always accompanied by skin symptoms?

In the major studies of anaphylaxis in the medical literature, 80 percent of patients had some type of skin or mucous membrane symptom, typically itchiness around the mouth and lips, hives, swelling of the mouth, tongue and face, flushing, and generalized itching. An anaphylactic reaction usually begins with skin symptoms and then rapidly evolves into a systemic reaction with other organ systems. However, up to 20 percent of patients with food and insect sting anaphylaxis do not have any skin symptoms at all, so the absence of any skin involvement does not rule out an anaphylactic reaction. I have seen a number of insect sting anaphylactic reactions begin with decreased blood pressure and shock first, only to be followed by hives afterwards.

### What is biphasic anaphylaxis?

Michael was on summer vacation with his family and had just had some ice cream when he felt ill, with vomiting and wheezing. His mother gave him his EpiPen right away and drove to the nearest hospital emergency room, which fortunately was close by. By the time they reached the hospital, his symptoms had resolved. He was given prednisone and observed for two hours. They concluded that the reaction was most likely due to the ice cream cross-contaminated with nuts and that the vomiting had expelled most of the allergen. Because he now appeared to be totally normal, he was discharged with a three day prescription for prednisone and Benadryl.

On their way home, still on the highway, Michael started to break out in hives and began wheezing again and complained that he couldn't breathe. Because they had used their only EpiPen and did not have a second one, he was treated with his albuterol inhaler and Benadryl, and luckily there was an urgent care clinic right off the highway at the next exit. Upon arrival, he was immediately treated with epinephrine and intravenous steroids. Because of the late-phase reaction, the decision was made to observe him overnight for any more allergic symptoms. He did well and went home the next morning.

Approximately five to 20 percent of people undergoing acute allergic reactions experience **biphasic anaphylaxis,** in which the initial symptoms are followed by a delayed wave of symptoms one to eight hours later. These symptoms are usually similar to the acute symptoms, with hives, swelling, gastrointestinal symptoms, wheezing, and decreased blood pressure. The mechanism of biphasic anaphylaxis may be continued absorption of allergen from the GI tract and/or the formation and release of additional chemical mediators triggering secondary responses. Having a biphasic reaction increases the severity of the reaction and the risk for a fatal outcome. Ninety percent of biphasic reactions occur within four hours, but the time course can be extended to eight to seventy-two hours after the initial reaction. The biphasic reaction does not respond to antihistamines. Steroid medications are prescribed to prevent biphasic anaphylaxis but, unfortunately, they may not be effective. Because the occurrence of biphasic anaphylaxis is unpredictable and medications may not be able to prevent it, intensive medical treatment in a hospital may be necessary.

I recommend that, if you experience anaphylaxis, use your epinephrine and then seek immediate medical attention at the nearest medical facility by contacting 911 or your local emergency medical services. Medical observation for biphasic anaphylaxis should be for at least a minimum of four to six hours. According to Dr. Hugh Sampson, most biphasic responses will occur within that critical time period. In a more recent review, Dr. Phil Lieberman of the University of Tennessee College of Medicine suggests an eight-hour observation period. Sometimes, in a very busy emergency department, you may be discharged before the four to eight hours are up. I suggest that, if you and your physician are unable to convince the emergency staff to have you stay longer, you do not leave the facility. Simply take a seat in the waiting area for the rest of the four to six hour time period. That way, if a delayed reaction does occur, you will still be able to receive prompt medical attention.

## Can severe anaphylaxis be predicted?

Richard had seen an allergist for asthma when he was a child. He had allergy testing then and recalled being told that he was allergic to cats, dogs, dust, and pollen. He never had any problems with food allergy. Two weeks ago, he collapsed while eating at a Chinese restaurant. He was brought to the nearest hospital emergency room and found to be in shock. Tests showed no evidence of a heart attack. His skin showed no evidence of any insect sting, and his lungs were clear with no asthma; he was on no medications. He recovered fully and was discharged in forty-eight hours. He was referred for allergy testing to rule out food anaphylaxis. Skin tests were positive to peanuts, cashews, and almonds. His wife remembered that, on that evening, they had ordered beef satay with peanut sauce and chicken with cashews.

There is unfortunately no available test to predict who is at risk for a life-threatening allergic reaction, short of doing an actual challenge test. The size of skin tests and the severity of positive RAST tests do not correlate with the risk of anaphylaxis. Anyone who is allergic can potentially undergo an anaphylactic reaction. Peanut reactions are often severe, even on the first exposure. Forty percent of first reactions to peanuts involve wheezing and respiratory distress. Eighty percent of peanut-allergic patients have had reactions involving difficulty breathing. Because of this, I prescribe EpiPen or Twinject to all my patients with peanut and nut allergies, regardless of history.

### What are the risk factors for fatal anaphylaxis?

There are four factors that increase the risk for a near-fatal or fatal anaphylactic reaction: (1) not receiving treatment with epinephrine or not receiving it in time; (2) a history of previous anaphylaxis, especially episodes accompanied by delayed or late phase reactions (**biphasic anaphylaxis**); (3) having peanut and tree nut allergy; (4) a history of asthma. Being extra careful about following your restriction diet, especially when eating outside your home, and having your epinephrine autoinjector with you at all times is essential.

Ninety percent of fatal reactions occur within the first hour after exposure. If epinephrine is administered within minutes of the exposure, the outcome is significantly better. If you have asthma, make sure that it is under good control, and be sure that you have your asthma rescue inhaler with you at all times.

Several studies show that up to 30 to 35 percent of anaphylactic reactions may be severe enough to require at least a second dose of epinephrine. Therefore, you should keep at least two EpiPens or one Twinject, which contains two doses of epinephrine, on your person. In addition, having two doses ready will cover the possibility that the first dose may misfire or be defective. Because one epinephrine dose may last only twenty to thirty minutes at the most, in the case of a severe, prolonged reaction or in the event of a delayed reaction, be prepared to administer a second dose. All peanut-allergic individuals and their families should be prepared to treat anaphylaxis. Because there is no cure for peanut allergy, strict avoidance and preparedness are the keys to management.

### What is the treatment for anaphylaxis?

Dennis knew as soon as he bit into the cookie that something was wrong. His lips and the inside of his mouth began to itch and burn. His tongue and throat felt swollen within a minute, despite his downing a glass of water. He knew that this was serious, and he had to get to his car where he kept his EpiPen. Running out the door, he started to wheeze with each breath. He was fumbling for his keys when he felt he was going to pass out. The last thing he remembered was injecting himself in the thigh with the EpiPen as he fell to the pavement.

---

Clearly, avoidance is the best treatment plan. Documenting the exact allergens responsible for the reactions, and gaining understanding and insight into where the allergens are located (and hidden!), is the key to any successful plan. This is the subject of another chapter, which will deal with this crucial matter in detail. Once the allergic exposure has occurred and symptoms follow, certain steps need to be followed to prevent severe, potentially fatal anaphylaxis.

The first step is to recognize the signs and symptoms of anaphylaxis and to determine that anaphylaxis has occurred. Once you determine that the person is having anaphylaxis, epinephrine must be given immediately. If the reaction is severe and there is no immediate improvement, then assess for the "ABCs" of CPR (cardiopulmonary resuscitation) taught in basic first aid classes: "Airway, Breathing, Circulation." If the person feels dizzy or faint, lying down with the feet elevated will maintain blood pressure and blood flow to the heart and brain.

---

### The ABCs of CPR

**Step 1:** Check for unresponsiveness. Call 911.

**Step 2:** Tilt head back and listen for breathing. If not breathing, pinch nose, cover mouth with yours, and blow. Watch for the chest rising. Give two breaths, one second for each breath.

**Step 3:** If patient hasn't responded, start chest compressions, pushing down 1.5 to 2 inches at the breast bone. Do thirty chest compressions followed by two breaths, repeating this cycle until help arrives.

---

Epinephrine given by intramuscular injection is the only drug treatment for anaphylaxis. Epinephrine is given for any symptoms that extend beyond the skin, such as swelling, choking, obstruction of breathing through the throat or the lungs, wheezing, dizziness, vomiting, diarrhea, abdominal pain, and rapidly progressive hives spreading in a generalized manner. Uterine cramping and a feeling of "impending doom" have also been observed as signs of anaphylaxis. Any of these symptoms can be a sign of a potentially life-threatening reaction.

Epinephrine is the same chemically as the hormone that our adrenal glands produce in response to stress. It increases heart rate and blood pressure and, in general, prepares the body for trouble. In the event of an acute asthma attack caused by a food-allergy reaction, administration of epinephrine will quickly reverse bronchospasm and stop wheezing. Epinephrine will also stop the leakage of fluid from blood vessels and restore normal blood pressure and heart function. These actions occur in seconds and are life-saving. Epinephrine has a short duration of action and will usually wear off in twenty minutes. Therefore, in a severe prolonged episode of anaphylaxis, it might be necessary to repeat the epinephrine injection. If the symptoms have not responded to the first epinephrine injection and you are getting worse, the second injection can be given after five minutes.

The use of epinephrine should be followed by immediate transport to the nearest medical facility for continuation of definitive treatment, monitoring, and follow-up. Epinephrine acts to stimulate the cardiovascular system, causing the common side effects of this drug, which are increased heart rate, increased blood pressure, and tremor of the muscles. In the setting of anaphylaxis, an immediate health threat, it is always better to use epinephrine early and to deal later with any transient side effects from the epinephrine.

Anaphylaxis cannot be treated, prevented, or "masked" by the use of antihistamines. Anaphylaxis is an explosive, rapidly progressive reaction that takes place in a matter of seconds to minutes, typically within an hour of allergen exposure. Epinephrine works in seconds and is the only effective treatment for acute anaphylaxis. Antihistamines such as Benadryl don't take effect for at least twenty to thirty minutes or longer, which is too late. Steroid medications such as prednisone take at least several hours to work and have not proven to be effective in preventing late phase anaphylactic reactions (biphasic anaphylaxis), even though they are commonly used for that purpose, as well as when there is an asthmatic component to the reaction.

Once epinephrine has been administered, call 911 for transport to the nearest medical facility. This is necessary for a four- to eight-hour observation period to monitor for any signs of biphasic anaphylaxis. Because late phase reactions can be more difficult to treat than immediate phase reactions and can sometimes fail to respond to treatment with epinephrine, you should only be observed in a hospital where you can be provided with specialized and intensive medical care in the event that these more severe and difficult reactions occur.

### Do all ambulances carry epinephrine?

Not all ambulances and emergency medical technicians (EMTs) have epinephrine or the training to use epinephrine. The EMTs that are able to give epinephrine have the highest training level; they are classified as EMT paramedics. The EMTs who have only the basic training may or may not be qualified and licensed to give epinephrine. This depends on what state you live in. Some states do allow for the EMT with basic training to assist the patient with his or her own EpiPen or Twinject. Contact your local ambulance and emergency services and find out who will respond to your emergency call and whether the responding EMTs will carry epinephrine and have the training to administer it.

FAAN has been instrumental over the past few years in raising public awareness of this problem, and their efforts have resulted in most states upgrading their EMT training to include epinephrine training and administration and having epinephrine available in all ambulances. As of early 2006, seven states (Alabama, Arkansas, Montana, Nevada, South Carolina, South Dakota, and Vermont) did not have most of their EMTs equipped and trained with epinephrine. Hopefully, with your efforts and those of FAAN, these states are working on changing their regulations and policies.

## When should antihistamines be used?

When only the skin is involved, a rapid-acting antihistamine is often all that is necessary. Antihistamines block the binding of histamine to tissue receptors, which is what causes the actual symptoms of allergy such as itching, redness, hives, and swelling. For the treatment of anaphylaxis, antihistamines should be given *after* the epinephrine has been administered. Antihistamines can be useful secondary medications in treating anaphylaxis, but epinephrine remains the only first line of treatment.

Examples of antihistamines available without prescription are diphenhydramine (Benadryl), loratidine (Claritin, Alavert), and chlorpheniramine (Chlortrimeton). Benadryl is commonly used for food-allergic reactions because it is very effective for skin reactions and works rapidly, usually within an hour. It is a very safe medication, suitable for use by young children and pregnant women. Its main side effect is drowsiness. Another effective antihistamine for acute allergic reactions is hydroxyzine (Atarax), which is available by prescription. It also has drowsiness as its main side-effect. It is a good idea to have the liquid formulations of either Benadryl or Atarax on hand because these are more rapid-acting than tablets, which need to be digested before entering the bloodstream.

The newer non-sedating antihistamines, such as loratidine (Claritin), desloratidine (Clarinex), fexofenadine (Allegra), and cetirizine (Zyrtec), are also effective, but they may not have as rapid an onset of action, so they may not be as useful in an acute, potentially severe reaction. They are probably of more use for preventive therapy of hay fever or chronic hives, when a daily maintenance antihistamine is required.

Antihistamines relieve the discomfort from skin symptoms, any rash such as hives or flare-ups of eczema, itching, and runny nose, sneezing, red watery eyes, and cough from post-nasal drip.

## Should I use my asthma inhaler if I wheeze from an allergic reaction to food?

Robert is a six-year-old boy with mild asthma since infancy who developed peanut allergy at age one when he had hives and wheezing while eating at a Chinese restaurant. There was apparently some peanut in a chicken dish that he ate. He was treated with Benadryl and nebulized albuterol with clearing of his symptoms. At age two, he ate some candy containing peanut and had facial swelling with vomiting. These symptoms cleared with Benadryl and nebulized albuterol. RAST testing to peanut at that time was highly positive as well as positive to egg, wheat, and soy. A few years later, he was exposed in school to a bird feeder that was made with peanut butter. He developed wheezing and swelling of his eyes and was treated again with Benadryl and his albuterol inhaler. Both of Robert's parents are doctors and were somewhat surprised when I disagreed with the treatment of Robert's wheezing from peanut allergy with Benadryl and inhaled albuterol. When I discussed wheezing in the context of a food reaction as anaphylaxis and not asthma, they realized their mistake. Subsequently, when Robert had an episode of wheezing, hives, and facial swelling at school, he was treated with his EpiPen.

---

Wheezing, chest tightness, coughing, and shortness of breath all are symptoms of asthma, but when they occur as an allergic reaction to food, you are dealing with anaphylaxis. Therefore, the treatment for these breathing problems is epinephrine, not albuterol. The mistake of using the albuterol inhaler first is a very common one because, for most asthmatic patients, the reaction may feel like a typical asthma attack, and the first impulse is to treat wheezing with the inhaler. You have to be very aware of what has triggered your chest symptoms: your environmental allergies, the common cold, or having eaten a food to which you're allergic. This is a key distinction to make especially if you have asthma and food allergies, which is a very common combination. Studies show that not only is having asthma a risk factor for fatal anaphylaxis, but having food allergy increases the risk of fatal asthma. These are good reasons, if you are asthmatic, to have your asthma under good control.

Once the symptoms of wheezing and anaphylaxis have been treated with epinephrine, asthma treatment can be administered for relief of obstructed breathing. When wheezing occurs as a result of bronchospasm and narrowing of the airways in the lungs, inhaled medications, called bronchodilators, can be used to reverse this narrowing and restore normal breathing. These inhaled medications are part of the standard therapy for asthmatic patients. However, if you have food allergies but not asthma, inhalers might not necessarily be prescribed, unless you have a history of wheezing. Asthma inhalers,

---

## Special Caution for People on Beta Blockers

Beta blockers are a class of drugs used commonly in the treatment of hypertension, migraine headaches, and glaucoma. They are also used in the follow-up care of heart attack patients and after surgery. Unfortunately, beta blockers block the beneficial actions of epinephrine on heart and lung tissue, thus rendering it ineffective in the treatment of anaphylaxis. Therefore, if you are taking a beta blocker such as Inderal, Tenormin, Timolol, Timoptic, Toprol, or Lopressor for hypertension, heart disease, glaucoma, or migraine headaches, consult your physician for appropriate alternative medicines. Beta blockers also worsen asthma control and are contraindicated in patients with asthma.

---

especially over-the-counter inhalers such as Primatene Mist, are inappropriate in the treatment of anaphylaxis and should not be used to treat anaphylaxis without also administering epinephrine.

## What is the difference between EpiPen and Twinject?

Epinephrine is available by prescription as a preloaded autoinjector, as either EpiPen or Twinject, a new device that became available in 2005. These are user-friendly, disposable devices easily used by most people. The added feature of Twinject is that it contains a second pre-loaded dose of epinephrine. The second epinephrine dose in Twinject is a preloaded syringe instead of an autoinjector dose, so there is some additional training necessary to use it. The EpiPen is designed so simply that the patient does not need to measure doses or even see the needle of the injector. The device is activated by pressing it into the thigh muscle and held in place for a few seconds to allow the medicine to penetrate. Twinject's first dose is activated in the same way as the EpiPen's. The second dose is a preloaded syringe with a visible needle, which is injected into the thigh muscle, and the plunger is depressed to complete the injection.

Be prepared to treat an anaphylactic reaction with two doses of epinephrine because four studies of anaphylaxis have shown that between 16 to 36 percent of acute anaphylactic reactions may require a second dose. The requirement for the additional epinephrine dose was for the initial reaction, not for a biphasic reaction. In one study of sixty-four anaphylactic reactions, 3 percent of patients required a third dose. Also, because it is a mechanical device, if the first dose fails to activate or is improperly discharged, an available second dose would be important to have as a precaution. The Twinject, by containing two doses in the same device, is more compact, weighs less than 2 EpiPens, and is perhaps more convenient than carrying two EpiPens. However, the second Twinject dose is a preloaded syringe with a visible needle, not an autoinjector dose, and it does require two additional maneuvers to administer. I suggest that you ask your physician to show you both devices, and you can try using the trainers, to get a feel for which you prefer. Ultimately, the important thing to remember is that whichever epinephrine autoinjector you have, know how to use it and when to use it, and have that second dose available.

## How to Use Your EpiPen

Remove the gray safety cap. Hold the EpiPen with the black tip against the fleshy outer portion of the thigh. Do not cover the end of the EpiPen with your thumb! Apply moderate pressure, and hold for ten seconds. Pushing the EpiPen against the thigh releases a spring-activated plunger, pushing the concealed needle into the muscle and discharging a dose of epinephrine. You can use the EpiPen directly through clothing. Upon removing the EpiPen after the injection, you will see a short needle protruding. The beneficial effects of the drug will be felt within seconds. The most common side effects are a temporarily more rapid heartbeat and slight nervousness.

## How to Use Your Twinject

Pull off the green cap first and then the red cap. Place the gray cap against the outer thigh and press down to discharge the epinephrine dose. Hold the Twinject in place for ten seconds and then remove. If the symptoms do not improve after five minutes, administer the second dose. Unscrew the gray cap and pull the syringe from the barrel by holding the blue collar at needle base. Slide yellow collar off the plunger. Inject the syringe needle into the outer thigh, and depress the plunger all the way then remove syringe.

## What is the correct dose of epinephrine to use?

Both the EpiPen and Twinject contain 0.3 mg of epinephrine, while the EpiPen Jr. and Twinject 0.15 mg contain 0.15 mg of epinephrine. The dosage of epinephrine to use is based on body weight. Doctors refer to a formula 0.01 mg per kg body weight, which works out to a weight range of 33 to 66 pounds for the EpiPen Jr./Twinject 0.15 mg and greater than 66 pounds for the EpiPen/ Twinject. Interestingly, this formula is not based on clinical studies but has been in the medical literature for many decades. As a result, there is variability in the doses prescribed for patients; the instructions for epinephrine prescribing gives the doctor flexibility in dosing based on the particular patient's medical history.

For example, for a child with a history of anaphylaxis and asthma, I would prescribe the EpiPen at a weight of 45 pounds whereas for another child who has never had any reactions at all, I would prescribe the EpiPen at a weight of 66 pounds. On average, for children who weigh less than 50 pounds I prescribe EpiPen Jr. or Twinject 0.15 mg, and for children weighing more than 50 pounds and for adults, I prescribe EpiPen or Twinject.

For young children weighing less than 33 pounds, according to the formula of 0.01 mg per kg body weight, the EpiPen Jr. or Twinject 0.15 mg would technically be an overdose. Because there is no epinephrine autoinjector containing less than 0.15 mg, one option to get the exact dose is to have the epinephrine manually drawn up in a syringe. Unfortunately, this technique is very difficult to learn, and in the actual event of anaphylaxis, studies show that mistakes in drawing up the correct dose and in the administration of the syringe are common. Most experts recommend prescribing the EpiPen Jr. or the Twinject 0.15 mg to children weighing less than 33 pounds despite the potential for a higher dose. The side effects of too much epinephrine are typically high heart rate, trembling, headache, and elevated blood pressure, somewhat like the effects of drinking too much coffee. Like caffeine effects, however, these symptoms wear off after fifteen to thirty minutes, are not harmful in children, and are generally well tolerated. When dealing with life-threatening anaphylaxis, I prefer to err on the side of giving too much epinephrine rather than taking the chance on the dose being given incorrectly or not given at all. The company that makes Twinject (Verus Pharmaceuticals, San Diego, CA) is working on an infant dose autoinjector, Twinject 0.1 mg, which would be a more appropriate dose for infants weighing 22 pounds to 33 pounds. This additional option will allow the infant and toddler to be treated for anaphylaxis with fewer potential side effects.

The EpiPen delivers only a single dose, so multiple EpiPens have to be available if more than one dose is needed. Because epinephrine has a 15- to 20-minute duration of action, prolonged, severe episodes of anaphylaxis may require repeat doses. Epinephrine can be repeated in as soon as five minutes if the anaphylactic episode does not respond to the first dose. The Twinject device makes the second dose conveniently available in the same device if the need arises. These devices are easy to use, and a school-age child can be taught how to use them with minimal effort. The EpiPen and Twinject both look like large fountain pens and fit in a shirt pocket. The epinephrine devices need to be with you or your child at all times, particularly when unanticipated allergen exposure is likely, such as when eating outside your home or in school. Most elementary schools require the epinephrine be kept in the nurse's office, so there must be a good plan for the student to have immediate access to the medicine when the nurse is unavailable. Some schools allow the epinephrine to be handed off from teacher to teacher as the students change classes. Most high schools allow for students to carry their epinephrine and self-administer medication with authorization from a physician.

In summary, if you were to ever experience anaphylaxis, the symptoms could be explosive and rapid, evolving in a matter of seconds to minutes. The only drug that will work quickly enough to reverse this and save your life is epinephrine by injection. It is the only drug that can simultaneously reverse airway narrowing, tissue swelling, and cardiovascular shock. Antihistamines work much more slowly and have no life-saving properties, but they do effectively reduce the discomfort of itching and hives. Antihistamines *never replace* the use of epinephrine in acute anaphylaxis. Steroids are prescribed to prevent the development of biphasic reactions that can occur hours after the initial reaction, but because they are not always effective, it is best to be observed in a medical facility for at least four to six hours. In the treatment of anaphylaxis, it is better to err on the side of giving epinephrine than not giving it.

All physicians are well qualified in the diagnosis and management of anaphylaxis, so if you ever have a severe reaction, use your epinephrine and then go to nearest emergency facility for treatment. *Early recognition and early treatment are the keys to the successful management of anaphylaxis.*

### How often can the epinephrine dose be repeated?

Although a dose of epinephrine acts in seconds and lasts fifteen to twenty minutes, for a very severe anaphylactic reaction, a conventional dose may be ineffective or only partially effective in reversing the symptoms. According to the most recently published guidelines for the treatment of anaphylaxis, epinephrine can be repeated every five to fifteen minutes, depending on how quickly the reaction is responding to treatment. Furthermore, the current treatment guidelines give a doctor the flexibility to give epinephrine even more frequently based on his or her clinical assessment of the situation. Obviously, an anaphylactic reaction that hasn't responded to one or two doses of epinephrine requires intensive medical care and treatment in a medical facility, and emergency medical services hopefully would have arrived by the time you have given the first dose. If you are in a remote area where you cannot be reached by emergency services within fifteen or twenty minutes, you do need to be prepared with multiple EpiPens or Twinjects.

## Would giving epinephrine unnecessarily cause harm?

The side effects of epinephrine are rapid heart rate, trembling, headache, elevated blood pressure, turning pale, and nausea. These side effects usually last for a relatively short time, fifteen to thirty minutes, and have no lasting effect. They are similar to the effects of caffeine. In young healthy individuals, these effects are generally well tolerated. So, if there is uncertainty as to whether or not to give the EpiPen or Twinject, it is better to err on the side of giving it because the risks of not treating anaphylaxis are far greater than the transient side effects of the epinephrine.

For the special case of patients with a history of heart disease, particularly older patients with coronary artery disease or a history of heart attacks, epinephrine can potentially narrow the coronary arteries and trigger a heart attack.

This conflict of medical problems does occur. I have some adult patients with a history of both heart disease and bee sting anaphylaxis. If they are stung, they need to use their epinephrine to prevent an anaphylactic reaction. I tell them that if they don't use it, they could die from the bee sting. If using the epinephrine results in a heart problem, we can treat the heart attack, but we can't treat them if they are dead from the bee sting. Again, this type of situation is uncommon, particularly in the case of peanut allergy, which typically affects younger, otherwise heart-healthy people.

## Can epinephrine be given in any other form besides injection?

Inhaled epinephrine has been available as Primatene Mist, an over-the-counter asthma inhaler. In studies using Primatene Mist for the treatment of anaphylaxis, doses of fifteen to thirty puffs are needed to reach the equivalent dose of 0.3 mg epinephrine by injection. Dr. Estelle Simons and her colleagues studied whether children could use the epinephrine inhaler and found that only 20 percent of children were able to use the right number of puffs necessary to treat an ana-phylactic reaction. Eighty percent complained of a bad taste and difficulty taking ten to twenty puffs at one time. The study concluded that inhaled epinephrine is an unreliable way to treat anaphylactic reactions in children. Furthermore, the FDA is considering taking Primatene Mist off the market in the near future, which would elim-inate that option anyway.

Recently, Dr. Simons and her group published a study using a new rapidly disintegrating epinephrine tablet administered under the tongue for the treatment of anaphylaxis. The study was per-formed in rabbits and found that the tablets were easy to administer and achieved the same blood levels of epinephrine as injected epi-nephrine. This form of epinephrine may become a viable alternative to injected epinephrine in its ease of use. In addition, more precise doses can also be given according to the patient's age and weight.

CHAPTER 4

# PEANUT EXPOSURES

## What is the smallest amount of peanut
## that can cause an allergic reaction?

Daniel was only three months old when his parents realized that he was allergic to peanuts. He was still exclusively breast fed and had never been exposed to peanuts before. His father had been cracking and eating shelled peanuts while watching television. When Daniel cried, his father picked him up. Afterward, his father was surprised to see a swollen, red, hivelike imprint of his hand on Daniel's back.

---

In most peanut-allergy studies, the lowest doses of peanut provoking reactions was in the range of 50 to 100 milligrams (mg) administered in capsule form. To give you an idea of how small a weight this is, 1 ounce weighs approximately 30 grams and 1 mg is 1/1000 of a gram. An average peanut weighs approximately 500 to 800 mg, or half to three-quarters of a gram. This means that one-fifth to one-tenth of a peanut can cause a reaction. Hourihane addressed this issue of how small a dose of peanut people will react to in a study published in 1997. He and his colleagues in Southampton, England, challenged fourteen peanut-allergic patients with doses of peanut ranging from 10 micrograms (µg) to 50 mg. Remember, one microgram is one-thousandth of a milligram, or one-millionth of a gram! The peanut was administered in the form of peanut flour in gelatin capsules. Six of these patients had reacted to crude peanut oil, indicating a very high degree of sensitivity. Only nine reacted to 50 mg, the highest dose in the study. No patient reacted to 10 to 50 µg of peanut protein. The lowest dose causing any allergic symptoms was 100 µg, in two patients who had mild subjective oral symptoms. The lowest dose of peanut protein causing observable allergic symptoms was 2 mg, a quantity easily reached by inhaling peanut dust. Two mg is approximately 1/250th of an average peanut.

Wensing and colleagues performed double-blinded placebo controlled challenges on 26 peanut-allergic adults with increasing doses of peanut to establish a threshold dose of reactivity. Threshold doses for allergy symptoms ranged from 100 µg up to 1 g of peanut protein. Fifty percent of the study subjects reacted to 3 mg of peanut protein, which is approximately equivalent to 1/50 of a peanut. The lowest level of peanut protein at which no adverse effect was observed was 30 µg.

That microgram amounts of protein can induce allergic symptoms suggests that the potential for contamination is quite high and that quality controls in the food processing, packaging, and manufacturing industry, as well as in restaurants and food preparation establishments, need to be reexamined. Peanut-allergic consumers of these goods and services need to be always wary of and vigilant about the potential for "hidden allergens" occurring in tiny amounts in processed foods and eating establishments. This may well apply to other highly allergenic food proteins as well, such as tree nuts, fish, and shellfish.

### What is "airborne" peanut allergy?

Elisa, age seven, had only mild asthma symptoms, usually sports-related. She was allergic to peanuts but knew to stay away from them. Riding home from school one afternoon, she was seated next to her best friend, who had unwrapped the peanut butter and jelly sandwich she hadn't had time to eat in school. Elisa didn't think anything of it, but by the time she got home 15 minutes later, she was having an asthma attack and needed to use her inhaler.

---

Allergic reactions are caused by food proteins. Proteins can become airborne when the food is vaporized by heat or when the food is ground up or pulverized. At cooking temperatures, the proteins convert from solid phase to a vapor phase. When this vapor is inhaled, it can cause allergic symptoms. Cooking fumes, in particular, have been cited as triggers of asthma attacks and runny nose symptoms. The cooking odors of fish and shrimp have been cited as triggers of occupational asthma for workers in the seafood industry. The cooking vapors of eggs and steamed milk have also been reported to cause allergic reactions. Other airborne food particles from cooking that may cause reactions have included string beans, lentils, and meats. In a similar setting, if peanuts, peanut butter, peanut oil, or peanut sauces are being cooked, the vapors emanating from the cooking can cause allergic reactions.

Airborne peanut exposure can also occur when enough peanut particles are released from vacuum-packed peanut snacks in a pressurized airline cabin with a recycled air ventilation system. In this situation, there is the potential for allergic reactions from inhaling the peanut particles. The third example of airborne peanut exposure is at a baseball park where peanuts and peanut shells are everywhere, especially on the ground being crushed underfoot into small particles that are easily taken up by wind currents and become airborne. A gust of wind can expose someone to this "peanut dust" and cause allergic reactions.

Now, what types of symptoms can you expect from this type of airborne exposure? Usually the symptoms consist of itchy eyes and runny nose, not unlike an airborne exposure to pollen, animals, or dust in someone with hay fever and environmental allergies. For anaphylaxis to occur, the peanut protein must be ingested, come in contact with the mucous membranes of the mouth, or find its way into the bloodstream, such as through a cut in the skin. An open jar of peanut butter at room temperature should have no significant vapor phase and therefore should not be a source of airborne peanut protein.

### Does having severe peanut allergy mean I can have an airborne reaction?

Airborne peanut allergy describes the route of exposure to the peanut allergen, not the severity of your peanut allergy. All patients with peanut allergy, regardless of severity, can have reactions to peanut vapor from cooking, from peanut particles from crushed peanuts, or from peanut particles in the recycled air of an airliner cabin. The severity of a person's allergy is determined by his or her history of previous allergic reactions. If the previous reactions were anaphylaxis, the person would be considered to have a more severe peanut allergy than someone who only has had mild skin symptoms, such as itching and rash.

Having had an airborne reaction does not necessarily constitute having a severe allergy; conversely, having a severe peanut allergy does not necessarily mean that you have had an airborne reaction. Remember, most airborne exposures result in itchy eyes and runny nose, and anaphylaxis is rare. The reactions that peanut-allergic patients experience can vary from exposure to exposure: one time, an exposure may cause a mild reaction and the next time, the same exposure might cause a more severe reaction. The severity of reactions and the risk of anaphylaxis are not predictable by skin testing or RAST tests. Indeed, it is this uncertainty that makes peanut allergy such a concern for all of us and why such care in avoidance and prevention is so important.

## Can the odor of peanuts cause an allergic reaction?

Another way of asking this question is, "Is smelling the odor of peanut butter equivalent to the different types of airborne exposures described in the previous section?" There are reports in the medical literature of people experiencing allergic reactions merely from smelling the odor of foods they are allergic to. Dr. John Carlston, an allergist from Eastern Virginia Medical School, reported in 1988 on a twenty-eight-year-old woman who had sneezing and itching reactions to the odor of peanut and peanut butter since childhood. The allergy worsened with age and reached a point where nasal symptoms occurred when peanuts were opened on another floor at the far end of the building from where she was located. Subsequently, she developed severe nasal symptoms and an asthma attack while on an airplane after peanuts were served on the flight.

There are other similar anecdotal reports of allergic reactions to the smell of peanuts or peanut butter in medical literature. In 1996, Dawe and Ferguson reported on four patients from the U.K. with anaphylaxis to "airborne peanut vapor," a phrase that they used to mean smell. Remember, however, that allergic reactions to food are triggered by food proteins only—the chemicals responsible for a substance's odor are called "volatile organic compounds." They are not proteins and are therefore incapable of causing allergic reactions. For peanuts, the volatile organic compounds causing its distinctive odor are called pyrazines.

Several years ago, a popular children's book had a "scratch and sniff" feature. On one page was a picture of a jar of peanut butter that, when scratched, emitted the distinctive odor of peanut butter. Naturally, there was great concern that this book could be dangerous for peanut-allergic children to smell. The book was subsequently sent to the University of Nebraska for chemical analysis by Dr. Steven Taylor, and sure enough, despite the odor of peanut butter, the book contained no peanut protein and thus posed no danger for peanut-allergic children.

The specific issue of whether peanut-allergic patients could react to the smell of peanut butter was examined in a well-designed study in 2003 by Dr. Simonte and his colleagues at Mount Sinai Medical Center. Thirty children with histories of severe peanut allergy, all with CAP RAST levels greater than 100 kU/L and with histories of reactions to smells, were entered in a placebo controlled double blinded experiment. The placebo used in this study was soy nut butter. Both the peanut butter and soy nut butter were disguised with mint and tuna to hide the real smell, as well as physically covered with gauze to hide its appearance. A measured amount of either the peanut butter or soy nut butter was placed 12 inches from the subject's nose for ten minutes. The subject was then observed for one hour in a normally ventilated room. There were no symptoms of any kind observed in any patient. This experiment conclusively demonstrates that the inhalation of peanut butter odor does not cause allergic reactions. Another study by Dr. Perry and colleagues from Johns Hopkins Medical Center analyzed the air around peanut butter, peanuts and peanuts being shelled, and found no detectable peanut protein in the air samples. While the testing methods might have been unable to detect very small amounts of airborne peanut protein, those small amounts would be unlikely to cause significant reactions and anaphylaxis.

How, then, do we explain the symptoms that patients experience when they smell peanuts and peanut butter? Hourihane from the U.K. believes that many reactions to the odor of peanut are "a psychological aversion and a method of self-defense against true allergic contact [rather] than allergic reactions actually mediated by small volatile proteins." He does, however, state that it is not proven that "extremely sensitive patients" would not react to the smell of peanuts" and this problem needs to be taken seriously, especially in enclosed spaces, such as airplanes that recycle air supply. Anne Muñoz-Furlong of the Food Allergy & Anaphylaxis Network says that the Medical Board of the Food Allergy & Anaphylaxis Network does not believe that the odor of peanut products would cause true allergic reaction, although it could clearly cause a panic reaction.

The physical reactions that people have experienced from smelling peanut may be conditioned physiological responses similar to the conditioning of the salivating dog to the sound of a bell in Pavlov's famous experiment. Almost any physiologic response can be conditioned, from rapid heart rate, flushing, itching, hives, and high blood pressure to wheezing. The peanut-allergic child has been taught from a very early age to stay away from peanut butter because of its life-threatening potential. The smell of peanut butter is therefore strongly associated with allergy as well as with danger and fear. The common symptoms of an allergic reaction can easily be conditioned over time. In addition, the symptoms of a panic or fear response can mimic the symptoms of a severe allergic reaction: increased heart rate, chest tightness, and difficulty breathing and talking. Unfortunately, the symptoms of a conditioned physiologic response and those of a panic attack may be very difficult to distinguish from a true allergic reaction. When in doubt, treat the reaction with appropriate allergy medications if the symptoms do not improve or subside with reasonable care and reassurance.

For patients and families who remain very concerned about inhalation exposures to peanut butter, I have conducted an "inhalation challenge" similar to the one that Dr. Simonte did, described in the previous section. I place an open jar of peanut butter in the same room as the patient, but I hide it behind something or place it behind the patient so it is out of sight. As a control, I use an open jar of jam or mustard. I have yet to have a patient experience a reaction. Once they see that there is no reaction, they feel reassured about being in the same room as peanut butter. Consider asking your allergist to conduct this type of challenge if the inhalation issue continues to bother your child.

## What are the risks associated with the different types of airborne exposures?

According to Dr. Robert Wood, director of the Pediatric Allergy Clinic at Johns Hopkins University Hospital, there are four levels of risk involving exposure to food. The greatest risk occurs during exposure to foods being cooked. The closer you are to the cooking, the greater the risk. The second level of risk occurs with the manipulation or disturbance of food, such as when peanut shells are crushed or swept. The third level of risk occurs with exposure to peanuts in a closed environment with recycled air, such as on an airplane. Although reactions do occur in this setting and have been reported in medical literature, as previously mentioned, it is still considered a rare problem for most people. The lowest level of risk occurs in the setting where food is being eaten but not cooked, such as in a dining hall or cafeteria, unless there is direct contact with the food.

To determine your level of risk, consider the exact conditions of your environment and your level of exposure and contact. How these conditions are modified will usually result from a negotiated compromise balancing your needs and the similar needs of other allergic people with the needs of the general public. The social and legal ramifications of potential situations in which public needs conflict with the needs of the allergic individual have not yet been fully played out. These issues will be addressed more fully in a later chapter.

### Can skin contact cause anaphylaxis?

The study performed by Dr. Simonte on the effect of peanut butter inhalation also examined the effect of skin contact with peanut butter on peanut-allergic children by the double blinded placebo controlled method. The same thirty children with severe peanut allergy were the subjects of the skin contact study. In this study, the placebo was soy nut butter that was mixed with a small amount of histamine to simulate the itchiness that would be associated with allergic skin contact from peanut butter. A measured amount of either peanut butter or the soy nut butter placebo was applied to the subject's back for one minute and then wiped off. The area of skin contact was then observed for one hour for any signs of allergic reaction. Three subjects (10 percent) had localized redness, five (17 percent) had localized itching without any visible redness or rash, two subjects (7 percent) had a single hive. None of these mild local reactions required any treatment. The authors concluded from these results that 90 percent of peanut-allergic individuals would not experience systemic or anaphylactic reactions to skin contact exposures to peanut butter, just mild local skin reactions.

# CHAPTER 5

# FINDING THE HIDDEN PEANUT PRODUCTS

### How can peanuts and peanut products be "hidden" in foods?

Katherine, age 18, was a nationally ranked squash player at Brown University. She was also very allergic to peanuts. After defeating the Wellesley College squash team, she and her teammates went out to a popular restaurant near the campus to celebrate. She ordered chili but did not inquire about nuts because she did not think chili would contain any nut or peanut products. After taking a few mouthfuls of the chili, she felt ill but was conscious and breathing. Her coach drove her to the home of a nearby local physician. He found her in shock. He injected her with epinephrine and called for an ambulance, which took her to the local hospital emergency department, arriving at 9:30 p.m. Efforts to resuscitate her failed, and she was pronounced dead at 10:55 p.m. The cause of the anaphylactic reaction was peanut butter used to thicken the chili.

---

Manufacturers are required to list ingredients on labels, especially highly allergenic foods such as peanut. Careful reading of labels is obviously helpful and important, but sometimes it is not enough.

The following terms on a package label may indicate the presence of peanut:

| | |
|---|---|
| Arachide (French) | Mandelona nut |
| Arachis oil | Marzipan |
| Artificial nuts | Mixed nuts |
| Beer nuts | Monkey nuts |
| Cacahueta (Spanish) | Nougat |
| Cold pressed, expelled, or expressed peanut oil | Nu-nuts |
| | Nutmeat |
| Goober peas (slang) | Peanut |
| Ground nuts | Peanut butter |
| Imitation nuts | Peanut flour |

The presence of tree nuts may be indicated by the following terms:

| | |
|---|---|
| Almonds | Marzipan/almond paste |
| Almond extract | Mashuga nuts (pecans) |
| Artificial nuts | Nougat |
| Brazil nuts | Nut butters (such as cashew butter) |
| Caponata | |
| Cashews | Nut meal |
| Chestnuts | Nut oil |
| Filbert/hazelnut | Nut paste (such as almond paste) |
| Gianduja (a mixture of chocolate cream and mixed nuts) | Pecans |
| | Pesto |
| Hickory nuts | Pine nuts (piñon, pignoli) |
| Imitation nuts | Pistachios |
| Indian nuts (pine nuts) | Walnuts |
| Macadamia nuts | |

For example, in the U.K. and Europe, peanut can be referred to as "groundnut," and peanut oil can be referred to as "arachis oil."

### What to Watch Out For

Peanut butter is a popular additive in cooking. Cooks favor its versatility because it adds extra flavor and texture to many dishes. Peanut butter is often used as a shortening or oil in recipes for many types of gravy. It can give a smoother texture to sauces. It is also used as a thickener for many recipes. Peanut butter has adhesive properties that allow it to be used to "glue down" the ends of egg rolls to keep them from coming apart. Peanuts, peanut oil, and peanut butter are commonly used in many international cuisines, particularly Asian cooking. Thai, Vietnamese, Chinese, Japanese, Indian, Indonesian, Mexican, African, and Ethiopian cooking are just some of the international cuisines in which peanut and peanut products play an important part.

For example, peanut butter is often used as a flavor enhancer in Chinese restaurants. Sauces and toppings can have finely crushed peanuts mixed in without any visible sign of them. Peanut sauce is often included as a hidden ingredient in chicken marinade. Peanut powder is a listed ingredient in some vegetable soup mixes. One brand of gourmet popcorn has peanut flavoring to enhance its special flavor. Peanut flour is used in certain brands of frozen dinners. "Slivered almonds" found on some baked goods may actually be made from raw peanuts because they are much cheaper. Peanuts can be re-flavored and pressed into other shapes, such as those of walnuts and almonds.

Crushed and finely ground peanut shells can be part of the stuffing material of bean bags, "draft blocker bags" that go under doors to prevent drafts, and similar items. Leakage or breakage of these items would lead to aerosol emission of highly allergenic peanut shell particles into the environment. One of my patients had a systemic reaction, with hives and runny nose, on exposure to a bird feeder. The ingredient label listed "peanut hearts." Some arts and crafts projects in schools use peanut butter as an ingredient. Read the labels on store bought arts and crafts projects carefully. Make your child's teacher aware that arts and crafts can be a hidden source of peanut exposure.

### The Importance of Cross-Contamination

Cross-contamination of food preparation equipment, utensils, and cookware is an important problem. Because of the demands of a busy restaurant kitchen, cookware and equipment are reused multiple times for many different entrees. Very small amounts of food that may not be obvious or visible to the cook, particularly oils and liquids, may be left behind to contaminate the next entree. Studies show that, for most food allergies, as little as 50 to 100 mg of food protein can be enough to cause an allergic reaction. However, because the peanut allergen is so potent, even 100 µg of peanut protein (ten times less than 100 mg) can induce allergic symptoms in patients.

Commercial food-manufacturing equipment can be a source of contamination. The production of nut butters, such as peanut and cashew, are often run on shared equipment. The nut and plain versions of many products are often processed on shared equipment. Fortunately, the food industry is now, for the most part, attuned to the reality of food-allergic consumers. It is usually standard procedure for equipment to be thoroughly cleaned between the production of different products, and many companies keep equipment exposed to peanut products separate from other pieces of equipment. Every once in a while, you hear of a company recall of a product contaminated by shared equipment in processing or packaging. Consumers should keep abreast of news reports and alerts from the food industry concerning product recalls and warnings. An excellent source of this information is the Food Allergy & Anaphylaxis Network, which publishes a newsletter and is also online (see Appendix A).

### Processing Additives

The term "hydrolyzed vegetable protein" used to be a commonly found ingredient on labels. Fortunately, manufacturers now are required to list the source of the vegetable protein, so the up-to-date labeling should read "hydrolyzed soy protein" or "hydrolyzed corn protein," etc.

A peanut-protein hydrolysate has been used as a foaming agent in soft drinks and as a whipping agent in confections. Hydrolyzed peanut protein is not commonly used in the U.S. because it is more expensive to produce than corn, soy, or wheat derivatives. However, in other parts of the world, peanut processing is less expensive, so hydrolyzed peanut protein may be more common in food manufactured overseas. Another problem with foods manufactured abroad is that labeling requirements are often different and less rigorous than those in the U.S. Therefore, it would be prudent to avoid hydrolyzed vegetable protein when traveling abroad or when buying international foods, which have become available in many supermarkets.

Ingredients such as oriental sauce, emulsifier, and "flavoring" also may contain peanut products. The possibility of cross-reaction with the legume lupine found in flour was discussed earlier. In general, be careful of processed foods, as they have a greater potential for containing undisclosed or hidden ingredients, including peanut products. Always read labels! I generally recommend limiting your intake of processed foods and eating only those with which you are very familiar. Learning to cook your own recipes with fresh and all-natural ingredients is not only allergy safe but otherwise healthier as well.

Intimidating as the above information may be, once you know what to look for and become familiar with certain brand names and ingredient lists, grocery shopping should be easier and more routine. But, again, don't forget to read those labels because food manufacturing and production methods do change! If you frequent a certain market, befriend the manager and have him or her special order items for you. If you frequent certain restaurants, let them become

## Foods to Be Cautious Of

Below is a list of some foods that peanut-allergic people should be cautious of. Find out as much as you can about the ingredient list of these foods because they might very well contain hidden peanut products. This is not an all-inclusive list, and you need to always read the labels of *all* foods.

| | |
|---|---|
| Baked goods | Ice cream |
| Baking mixes | Margarine |
| Battered foods | Marzipan |
| Biscuits | Nut butters |
| Breakfast cereals | Pastry |
| Candy | Satay dishes and sauces |
| Cereal-based products | Soups and soup mixes |
| Chili | Sweets |
| Chinese food | Thai food |
| Cookies | Vegetable fat and oil |
| Egg rolls | Vietnamese food |

familiar with you and your dietary needs. Reward these establishments with your business. Once you establish a plan and routine, eating in or out should remain a pleasurable and safe experience.

### Why aren't labels foolproof?

Joshua was diagnosed with milk protein allergy at age three months. He had severe eczema, hives, vomiting, and diarrhea with cow's milk formula and dairy products such as cheese, ice cream, and yogurt. His mother found that numerous food items she bought at the supermarket that were marked "dairy-free" and "Pareve" (Kosher designation for milk-free) caused allergic reactions. These items included baked goods, bread, and nondairy ice cream.

Labels obviously have to be read, and manufacturers are legally required to follow specific guidelines. The Two Percent Rule of The Code of Federal Regulations requires manufacturers to list ingredients that constitute more than 2 percent of the total weight, but they do not have to be listed in order by weight. Ingredients in flavors or spices are not required to be labeled, nor are incidental additives if they are not functional and are present in an insignificant amount (generally parts per million). An ingredient also can be listed as a "natural flavoring" to indicate a small amount of a food protein added for flavoring, without identifying the actual protein. An example of this is casein (a milk protein) added to canned tuna. There is an excellent article on this subject in the *Food Allergy News*, Aug.–Sept. 1996 issue, by Anne Muñoz-Furlong. On some occasions, a manufacturer will change ingredients without changing the labeling.

What is on labels can also be very misleading. For example, "nondairy" foods can contain milk protein; "egg substitutes" are low in cholesterol but are mostly egg white, which is the allergenic portion of egg; and Lactaid and other lactose-free milk lacks the sugar but has the same amount of milk protein. Thus, it is still most important to know all the possible "code words," listed previously, for peanuts, nuts, and allergenic foods that can make reading labels confusing. When in doubt, consult your allergist, consult the Food Allergy & Anaphylaxis Network, or call or e-mail the manufacturer or go to its Web site.

### Should I avoid foods that state "may contain traces of peanut" or "manufactured in a facility that processes peanuts and nuts"?

Unfortunately, there are no regulations in the food industry for these advisory labels on food products. This type of labeling is voluntary and varies from company to company. In most cases, the consumer is being warned that, due to the manufacturing or packaging procedures, there is the possibility of cross-contamination with peanuts contained in another food product produced in the same facility. My advice is to avoid buying that product and not to eat it.

### What is the Food Allergen Labeling and Consumer Protection Act?

On January 1, 2006, the Food Allergen Labeling and Consumer Protection Act (FALCPA) took effect. This new federal law requires the food manufacturer to disclose on ingredient labels the presence of the eight major food allergens in the product. These eight foods are milk, egg, wheat, soy, peanuts, tree nuts, fish, and shellfish. Any food ingredient that contains protein derived from the major food allergens, including additives and flavorings, are subject to this law. An exception to this is highly refined oil containing little or no protein.

The presence of the food protein can be listed as "contains," followed immediately by the food group (e.g. "contains peanut") or the labeling may list the ingredient immediately followed by the food source in parentheses (e.g., "natural flavors (peanut, almond)"). The common food allergens will be identified on the label in plain English—easy enough for a second grader to read. The intent of this law is to eliminate the confusion caused by the numerous terms used in the food industry for the many different food proteins, often obscure scientific terms familiar only to food scientists (e.g., ovalbumin is an egg protein). The hidden food allergens in natural flavors, spice blends, dyes, and colorings labels will be clarified or eliminated. Unfortunately, advisory or disclaimer-type labeling, such as "manufactured in a facility . . ." and "may contain . . ." will not be changed by this law, and food-allergic patients will still need to avoid food products that include it.

### Is peanut oil safe for peanut-allergic individuals?

Jane's favorite restaurants were Chinese, Thai, and Vietnamese, so when she was diagnosed with peanut allergy, she was crestfallen because she knew peanuts were a staple of Asian cooking. However, she discussed her problem with the managers of her favorite Asian restaurants, and they assured her that no peanuts would be used in cooking her meals. Unfortunately, she subsequently had anaphylaxis while eating a seafood dish at the Vietnamese restaurant. The entrée contained no peanuts or nuts of any kind, but one of the ingredients had been pan-fried in peanut oil before being added to the main dish.

---

Whether peanut oil is safe depends on how it is extracted. Peanut oil is extracted from peanuts by one of two methods. The chemical extraction method extracts the oil by using chemicals, such as hexane, and high-temperature distillation at temperatures of 300°F or higher. The expeller extraction method makes use of purely mechanical means, with an expeller device at temperatures from 150 to 200°F. This method has been referred to as "cold-pressed" because of the lower temperatures used, as compared to the chemical extraction method. Gourmet cooking oils often are extracted by this method because the oil is more flavorful and is considered more desirable because no chemicals are used to extract it. Once the oil is extracted, it can be further refined and purified by several processes that remove free fatty acids, soaps, peroxides, and other impurities that might affect flavor, appearance, or shelf life of the oil.

Several recent studies have analyzed the protein content of peanut oil that is extracted and purified through these methods. All studies show that chemically extracted and refined oils have negligible protein content and are not associated with reactions when consumed by peanut-allergic individuals. In contrast, the "cold-pressed" or expeller extracted oils contain peanut protein and can lead to allergic reactions. In general, the oils containing the highest protein concentrations—and, hence, the highest allergen levels—are the oils with the lowest levels of refinement.

Hourihane studied sixty peanut-allergic patients, challenging them with crude peanut oil and refined peanut oil. None of the sixty patients reacted to the refined peanut oil, whereas six (10 percent) reacted to the crude oil. Another study showed that one brand of crude peanut oil contained 3.3 µg of allergenic protein per milliliter of oil.

Another problem with cooking oils, particularly in a busy restaurant kitchen, is the risk of cross contamination when frying different foods in a shared deep fat fryer. In addition, it is common practice for the same frying pan to be used for multiple entrées, with the pan being wiped off between them.

Because of the significant variability of factory procedures, labeling ambiguities, and inconsistencies, you cannot assume that peanut oil is safe. As mentioned earlier, in manufacturing, peanuts and tree nuts are often processed on the same production lines, resulting in cross contamination of the final product. Because of these many possible problems and the severity of the risk involved, I advise peanut- and tree-nut-allergic patients to avoid all nut oils.

CHAPTER 6

# KEEPING SAFE IN A PEANUT-FILLED WORLD

### Should peanut snacks be banned from airlines?

Elaine is a thirty-four-year-old woman who has had a lifelong history of peanut allergy. She has had anaphylaxis when eating in restaurants on four occasions, despite always asking about the presence of peanuts in each entrée, and has used her EpiPen effectively each time. On a recent flight to Florida, she experienced sneezing, runny nose, and chest tightness when peanuts were served to the passengers seated in her row. She took Benadryl, which was sufficient to relieve her reaction, and did not need her EpiPen. She was moved to another part of the airplane and arrived safely at her destination with no further peanut exposures and no further reactions.

---

Peanuts have been served on airline flights since the 1950s. As the number of peanut-allergic passengers increased and reports of allergic reactions to peanuts on airlines occurred, complaints to the Department of Transportation prompted an inquiry into this matter. In 1996, the Mayo Clinic published an abstract demonstrating that peanut allergens could be found in airplane ventilation filters after 5,000 hours of flight time. Consideration of this study, as well as the Air Carriers Access Act of 1986, which guaranteed access to airlines for the disabled, prompted the department to issue a recommendation in August 1998. It said that all airlines should provide, on request, a three-row peanut-free buffer zone for a passenger with a medically documented peanut allergy.

This resulted in a huge outcry from peanut farmers and the politicians from the peanut-growing states, as well as from many members of the public who were offended by the fact that a small vocal minority was dictating policy. A number of airlines subsequently announced peanut-free flights on request for peanut-allergic passengers. The following table gives you an idea of the diverse polices of some airlines with regard to peanut-allergic passengers in 2006. The information in this table was compiled with the help of Terry Furlong and Christopher Weiss of FAAN and might have already been modified by the time you read this book. Policies are constantly subject to change due to reforms in the airline industry, so it is always wise to contact your airline well in advance before making reservations.

The debate that followed resulted in a reversal of this directive. The main objections were that (1) it was an excessive regulation on airlines and ignored the rights of the vast majority of air travelers, who are not peanut allergic; (2) the directive unfairly singled out one allergen, while ignoring other potentially important allergens; and (3) establishing peanut-free zones would establish a precedent for all forms of public transportation. Legislation was subsequently passed that prohibited funding for the Department of Transportation to implement its peanut-free zone directive but encouraged a scientific study of this problem. The lack of scientific studies demonstrating that airborne peanut allergen caused peanut-allergic airline passengers to have allergic reactions was cited as one of the main reasons for not mandating such strict recommendations.

Researchers at the Jaffe Food Allergy Institute in New York surveyed passenger reports of allergic reactions to peanuts on airlines

| Airline | Regularly serve peanuts? | Non-peanut snack or peanut buffer zone available upon advance request? |
| --- | --- | --- |
| Aer Lingus | No | |
| Alaska/Horizon | Yes | Yes |
| Alitalia | No | |
| Aloha | Yes | Yes |
| American | No | |
| America West | Yes | No |
| ATA | No | |
| British Airways | No | Yes |
| Continental | Yes | No |
| Delta | Yes | Yes |
| Japan Airlines | Yes | Yes |
| Jet Blue | No | |
| Northwest | No | |
| Southwest | Yes | Yes |
| Spirit | No | |
| U.S. Airways | Yes | No |
| United | No | |
| Virgin Atlantic | Yes | Yes |

Adapted with permission from The Food Allergy & Anaphylaxis Network Web site: www.foodallergy.org

and published their results in 1999. Sixty-two of 3,704 (1.65 percent) participants in the National Registry of Peanut and Tree Nut Allergy indicated that they or their children had had an allergic reaction to peanut while on a commercial airline flight. Forty-two respondents, with an average age of two years (range of age six months to fifty years) had an allergic reaction that began on an airplane. Thirty-five of the forty-two reacted to peanuts and seven to tree nuts, although three of these could have reacted to something that also contained peanuts. Twenty individuals reacted by ingestion, eight by skin contact, and fourteen by inhalation. The reactions usually occurred within ten minutes, and the severity of the reaction was worst for ingestion followed by inhalation, while the least severe reaction was by skin contact. During inhalation reactions, more than twenty-five other passengers were estimated to be eating peanuts at the time of reaction. Inhalation reactions usually consisted of upper airway symptoms, skin rash, or wheezing. The researchers felt that eleven of the fourteen inhalation reactions were very convincing for true allergic reactions, considering the timing and pattern of the reaction as well as the symptoms experienced. None of these inhalation reactions were life-threatening.

The people notified the flight crews only 33 percent of the time. Nineteen subjects received medical treatment in-flight, including epinephrine given to five, and an additional fourteen received treatment on arrival at the gate, including epinephrine given to one and intravenous medication to two.

Airlines have had epinephrine as part of their in-flight medical kits, as required by the Federal Aviation Agency, since 1986. It has been suggested to the airline industry that flight attendants be trained in the recognition of anaphylaxis and the use of epinephrine. Flight attendants should also be notified of passengers with life-threatening food allergies. Passengers should be warned that the airlines make no exceptional cleaning methods for flights. However, the airline might make allowances for allergic people to preboard so they can wipe down their immediate seating area. Passengers should be given the option of allergen-free meals or, ideally, peanut-free flights, if requested in advance. Passengers might be permitted, and encouraged, to bring their own meals if they so choose. Doing so would safeguard them from the possibility of cross contamination with other meals. None of these suggestions are policy yet, but lobbying and a strong group effort by enough people could certainly result in changes.

Ultimately, even banning peanuts and peanut products from all airline flights would not guarantee safety for the peanut-allergic patient at risk for anaphylaxis. Passengers, particularly children, often bring their own snacks and candies with them, and exposure and contact could easily result. There is certainly no way for airlines to prevent this from happening. The false sense of security that such flights might engender on the part of both the allergic passenger and the flight crew could end up causing more harm than good. Thus, the patient has to take the ultimate responsibility for being vigilant and prepared. The strategy of education and prevention is key. Patients, families, and their physicians can help airlines and their staff understand about peanut allergy, how to recognize and deal with the problems of contact and contamination, and how to handle an emergency allergy situation.

However, there is no substitute for prudent measures of prevention in dealing with this problem. Families need to always take the initiative and call ahead to inquire about the availability of peanut-free flights. It is a good idea to book the first flight of the day in the early morning, to improve the chances of flying on a freshly cleaned and vacuumed airplane. Ask for permission to preboard or board early to clean and wipe down the seating area. You or your child need to bring your emergency medications such as EpiPen or Twinject, a bottle of liquid Benadryl, and any other medications needed (asthma medications, eczema creams, etc.) in a carry-on bag for possible use during the flight. Remember, not only can checked luggage get lost, but it would be useless to have your medication under the plane if an allergic reaction occurred during the flight. Bring your own peanut-free food and snacks, so that you or your child don't get hungry and start being tempted by the peanut snacks and other foods of unknown composition. To keep your child from being bored and wanting to explore and wander all over the plane, bring enough toys, games, and other diversions to keep him or her busy.

### What are some of the problems facing the peanut-allergic infant and toddler?

Matthew is a two-year-old boy who first developed peanut allergy at age one year. He was exclusively breast fed until age twelve months and was not completely weaned until age eighteen months. He had developed eczema on his face, arms, and legs at two months. The eczema seemed to flare after his mother ate peanut butter and then nursed him. On his first contact with peanut butter, when he touched some on a cracker, he developed swelling of his face, followed by hives all over his body, and required Benadryl and epinephrine in his pediatrician's office. He has been kept on a strict peanut- and nut-free diet since then, and his mother eliminated peanut products from her diet. He had no problems until he was kissed by a relative who had just eaten a piece of candy containing peanut, and hives erupted where he was kissed.

---

Infants and toddlers have no control over their environment. How often they get into trouble is directly related to how carefully they are watched and cared for. A strict peanut-free diet and environment can be achieved for this age group more successfully than for any other age group. The ideal situation would be a baby that is exclusively breast fed by a mother who is herself adhering to a peanut-free diet in a household with no peanut products. Daycare would be avoided completely or at least delayed until age three.

Unfortunately, this ideal situation is seldom achieved and is a bit unrealistic. Siblings who are not old enough to understand that peanut butter can be dangerous should not be given peanut products except under supervision, so that accidental contacts with and exposures of the allergic child do not occur. The major mistakes occur when care of the child is given over to people who may not be as knowledgeable about peanut-free diets or who do not care to be. This is where you need to educate others about the seriousness of the allergy and how often peanut products can be "hidden." Any caretaker responsible for the baby needs to be fully trained in handling an emergency situation and in the use of epinephrine.

In the daycare setting with multiple children, it is the responsibility of the daycare provider to maintain a safe environment for all of his or her charges. How this is achieved certainly will vary from provider to provider. With very young active children, playing with and touching each other, it is quite difficult to monitor every child. Although skin contact typically results in minor skin reactions and not anaphylaxis, young children often put their fingers in their mouths, which can result in potentially more severe reactions. The chances for accidental contact and exposure increase with the number of children present. In an ideal world, the easiest way to maintain control would be to have a completely peanut-free environment. Because this is often difficult to achieve, however, it is up to you, as parents, to be in frequent contact with the daycare providers, to give them information, hands-on support, and help.

When looking at various daycare centers, inquire whether they have had children with allergic conditions, such as peanut allergy, and how the situation was handled. The more experience the daycare provider has had, the more confident you can be about the safety of your child. The Food Allergy & Anaphylaxis Network has a special educational package devoted to daycare centers and preschools. The Allergy and Asthma Foundation of America (AAFA) has a new program training childcare centers on dealing with food allergies, asthma, and other common allergy problems. Your local AAFA chapter will also direct you to the nearest support group and educational lectures given by community physicians and local experts. This is an invaluable source of information and a forum for sharing experiences and giving mutual support.

### How can my peanut-allergic child be kept safe at school?

Consider the following facts: Food allergies affect 8 percent of children under three and 6 to 8 percent of school-aged children. Eighty-five percent of children outgrow milk and egg allergies by age five, but only 20 percent outgrow peanut allergy by age six. The prevalence of peanut and tree nut allergies in children has doubled in the past five years. Peanut-allergic patients have accidental exposures and reactions every three years. Seventy-five percent of peanut-allergic reactions occur on the first known exposure. Twenty-five percent of epinephrine administrations in schools are for people who have never had food allergy or anaphylaxis. In the U.S., fatal food anaphylaxis occurs in 150 people each year, 90 percent from peanut and nut allergies. Fatal anaphylaxis occurs most often outside the home, in schools and restaurants. Given these statistics, every school needs to be prepared to deal with the problem of food anaphylaxis, especially from peanut allergy.

In 2001, following the death of a peanut-allergic student in Massachusetts, the Massachusetts Department of Education convened a Food Anaphylaxis Task Force, of which I was privileged to be a part. We discussed the growing problem of life-threatening food allergies in schools, the importance of making all schools aware of this problem, and the importance of having ways to prevent and manage anaphylaxis in schools. After meeting over the course of a year, the task force published in 2002, a seventy-six page set of guidelines for all schools in Massachusetts on "Managing Life Threatening Food Allergies in Schools." This detailed document addresses all aspects of managing food allergies in schools, including the action plan and recommendations for the classroom, cafeteria, school sports, playgrounds, extracurricular activities, school trips, and school buses. You can adapt sections from these guidelines for your child's action plan for school. You can view or download this document from the Web site of the Massachusetts Department of Education at www.doe.mass.edu/cnp. Many states and even schools from other countries have used these guidelines as a template for their own school policies.

The key points of the guidelines are to (1) identify the student with the food allergy to the school, (2) have a written emergency action plan in place for managing an anaphylactic reaction, and (3) have a written individual health care plan in place for the prevention and proactive management for the student in all the different school environments he or she may be in, from the classroom to the cafeteria to the bus to field trips. The emergency action plan is formulated by your physician with your input, based on your child's history, and specifies what symptoms to look for and what treatments are to be given, as well as contact information and directions for disposition following the reaction. The school nurse usually is responsible for implementing this plan in the event of an actual emergency. This is discussed in greater detail in the section on the school's responsibility to you.

The general principles of the preventive plan usually include the following:

1. The general principles of avoidance followed at home should be applied to the classroom, cafeteria, and all areas where the student may be. Nineteen percent of anaphylactic reactions in Massachusetts schoolchildren occurred outside the school building, on the playground, on the school bus to and from school, and on field trips.

2. For areas where food is consumed, hand washing, no food sharing, and the routine cleaning of surfaces where food is prepared and consumed to avoid cross contamination are practices that students and school staff need to learn and use.

3. For the classroom, students and staff need to become familiar with the concept of "hidden" peanut ingredients, not only in foods and but also in nonfood items that may be used in classroom projects in arts and crafts, math, and science. Reading the ingredient labels of foods, as well as other items such as bird feeders and pet feed, becomes an additional responsibility of the school teacher and staff.

4. There should ideally be a full-time nurse in any school where there are students with life-threatening allergies. If the school nurse is unable to be on site, she should be able to train a designated staff member in the management of anaphylaxis and the use of epinephrine.

5. Every student with life-threatening allergies needs to have an epinephrine autoinjector in the school. The epinephrine autoinjector needs to be accessible for quick access within several minutes of a reaction and kept in a secure but unlocked location.

6. Emergency communications between all the student's locations (classroom, cafeteria, gym, playground, etc.) and the school nurse and/or principal's office should be available. Students, families, teachers, and school staff should all be educated on food allergies, anaphylaxis, and general avoidance principles. The Food Allergy & Anaphylaxis Network is an excellent resource for educational programs for schools and provides many age-specific materials, including videos for children and a very useful kit for school staff and personnel.

### Should peanuts be banned from schools?

Mark, age five, is severely allergic to peanuts and has already had three episodes of anaphylaxis, one requiring hospitalization. He has been kept out of preschool because the family could not find a school that satisfied their stringent requirements. They are now about to enroll Mark in kindergarten and are requesting a letter of medical necessity from me and the pediatrician to order that his school prohibit peanuts and peanut products from Mark's classroom, as well as from the school cafeteria.

---

The social and legal aspects of this question are very similar to those of airline peanut exposure. Many preschools and some schools have in fact banned peanuts from the classrooms and cafeterias. Whether they do so largely depends on the number of students affected in the school and community, parents' efforts, and the willingness of the school system and community to make accommodations.

There are good arguments for both sides. Peanut allergy is a potentially life-threatening condition; it would make sense to eliminate any possibility of exposure in a setting with young children who cannot be expected to understand all the problems of management, let alone the implications of having a life-threatening reaction. On the other hand, without foolproof methods of guaranteeing peanut detection 100 percent of the time, there is no way to enforce a true "peanut-free" school. It would be difficult to do detailed inspections of all food brought into school by other students, assuming that everything had an ingredient label, and most families would not be expected to have adequate knowledge of peanut allergy to be able to make school lunches peanut-free—nor could they be expected to have that motivation. As with peanut-free flights, some also argue that a "false sense of security" results from a school that claims to be peanut-free, resulting in decreased vigilance and monitoring over time.

Another problem is that older children who never have to face dealing with "real-life" situations of hidden exposures, such as cross contamination, because they have been in peanut-free environments at home and at school, may be at a disadvantage when they go to college and eventually are on their own. In addition, there is the consideration of the children with other life-threatening food allergies. Do we also ban milk, eggs, wheat, soy, tree nuts, seafood, etc., from schools to accommodate these other students? These are by no means easy questions to answer and are the subject of many debates in local communities. Fortunately, most schools and families usually are able to agree on very practical school plans.

In most cases, compromise solutions are reached, such as having a peanut-free table in the cafeteria or a peanut-free room. Some schools have a designated peanut table or area where all the peanut products are eaten, leaving the rest of the cafeteria peanut free. These zone approaches are generally quite satisfactory because the actual risk in a dining hall with good ventilation and no exposure to the actual cooking fumes is very low, particularly for anaphylaxis. Of course, every effort needs to be made to minimize your child's sense of isolation; he or she should be able to pick several friends to sit at the peanut-free table.

In addition to cafeteria precautions, students are given age-appropriate education in allergy and what the consequences of anaphylaxis are. The dangers of sharing foods and snacks must be discussed. This education often must begin with the school nurse explaining these issues to administrative staff. For pre-schools and lower grade classes with very young, difficult-to-monitor children and classes with multiple peanut-allergic students, a peanut-free classroom might end up being an easier approach for teachers and staff.

The key to the success of any preventive plan is access to and availability of epinephrine. This can not be overstated. Without easy access to epinephrine in areas where food and eating occur, potential disaster awaits. This can be a problem, particularly for children who, because of their age, do not have permission to carry their epinephrine with them and are therefore dependent on the school nurse for their epinephrine.

Many schools have to share one nurse, so an individual school may only have the nurse there a few days each week. In this common situation, the nurse has the ability and legal authority in many states to train a designee in the use and administration of epinephrine. This designee can be a teacher, principal, secretary, or any individual in the school able and available to perform this crucial function in the absence of the school nurse. You need to know exactly what the school nurse's weekly schedule is and to whom she has designated the responsibility for administering epinephrine on the days she is not present in the school. You should have this plan in writing from the school nurse and principal.

### How can my peanut-allergic child be kept safe on a school bus?

Another issue is the school bus and whether the bus driver will be responsible for keeping the epinephrine and administering it in an emergency situation. Most school systems hire school bus companies on contract and do not own the buses, so the school does not usually have total control of the bus driver's responsibilities. The bus drivers may choose not to take direct responsibility for the specific medical problems of the students riding the bus. This is a potentially serious gap in your child's preventive plan, especially because the school bus is relatively unsupervised with respect to sharing food, snacks, and packed lunches from home.

A policy of no eating on the bus can prevent most food-related problems on the bus. For children with food allergies, seating them near the bus driver would allow closer supervision by the driver during the bus ride. All school buses should have a protocol to follow in the event of an emergency of any kind. The driver should have an emergency communications device to contact 911 or emergency medical services. You should find out what emergency protocol the school bus has in place. Be sure to raise this issue with the school because they do have responsibility for this part of the student's day as well.

## What are the most effective cleaning techniques for removal of peanut allergen?

A recent study showed that ordinary cleaning techniques are completely effective in removing peanut allergen from hands and surfaces. Using a sensitive laboratory test for measuring the major peanut protein Ara h1, Dr. Perry and her colleagues at Johns Hopkins University were able to measure the effectiveness of various cleaning techniques on the removal of peanut allergen from hands, tabletops, and other surfaces in school environments. After applying 1 teaspoon of peanut butter to the hands of volunteers, they washed their hands with plain water, antibacterial hand sanitizer, Tidy Tykes wipes, Wet Ones antibacterial wipes, liquid soap, and bar soap. Hand wipe samples taken before and after washing showed that all methods, with the exception of plain water and hand sanitizer, left no detectable peanut protein. This makes sense, as the hand sanitizer is alcohol-based and may not be effective in removing an oil like peanut butter. One teaspoon of peanut butter was applied to tabletops and allowed to air dry. The tabletops were then cleaned with plain water, dishwashing liquid, Formula 409 cleanser, Lysol sanitizing wipes, and Target brand cleaner with bleach. All cleaners were effective at removal of the peanut butter, with the exception of dishwashing liquid.

The investigators then paid surprise visits to six preschools and schools. Two of the schools had peanut-free tables or peanut-free food preparation areas and one school was completely peanut-free. None of the eating or food-preparation areas had detectable peanut protein, including nine samples from designated peanut-free areas. None of the desks sampled had any detectable peanut protein. Only one of thirteen water fountains had detectable peanut protein at a very low level. The investigators concluded that, under normal circumstances of hand washing and cleaning methods with common cleaning agents, school cafeteria tabletops and desktops

## Food Allergy and the Law

There have been cases of daycare centers and preschools denying admission to food-allergic children or refusing to allow the administration of epinephrine. *Food Allergy News* has followed the issue of food allergies and the apparent violation of the Americans with Disabilities Act (ADA) in several articles (1997;6(3):3, 1999;8(6):7). There is ongoing litigation involving a number of these cases. The ADA does require the daycare centers to "reasonably modify their policies, practices or procedures when the modifications are necessary to afford goods, services, facilities, privileges, advantages, or accommodations to individuals with disabilities, unless the public accommodation can demonstrate that making the modification would fundamentally alter the nature of the goods, services, facilities, privileges, advantages, or accommodations."

The Supreme Court recently ruled that the ADA does not cover individuals with disabilities that can be corrected or reversed with medical treatment. They felt the intent of the ADA was not to cover "common, correctable impairments and that the person must be limited presently, not potentially or hypothetically." Food-allergic individuals were not specifically dealt with in this ruling, but food anaphylaxis is neither "common" nor "correctable." How the food-allergic patient and the schools are affected will become clearer as legal precedents are set with the cases currently pending in the courts.

are unlikely to be significant sources of exposure to peanut proteins. This study is of great reassurance and reinforces the importance of hand washing and cleaning surfaces of tables and desks in students' school management plans.

## What is the responsibility of the school to your peanut-allergic child?

Nora, age five, is asthmatic and had anaphylaxis to peanut butter when she was eighteen months old. She has had hives from being kissed and from contact with playground equipment and toys. She is now enrolling in kindergarten, and the parents are asking my help in filing a "504 Individual Health Care Plan." The school district's attorney has asked me whether the family's request for a special aide to accompany her on the school bus and in the classroom is medically necessary.

A federal law, Section 504 of The Rehabilitation Act of 1973, states that schools must provide medical attention to children who need it and that budgetary cutbacks are not an acceptable excuse not to do so. The school has responsibility for the child's medical needs during the entire time the student is in attendance at school. State and federal law require that parents provide the school with written documentation of the child's allergies and the physician's signed treatment plan and procedure to follow in the event of a reaction.

The school nurse, or his or her designee, will implement the medical plan. The plan should be very specific and list the signs and symptoms to look for during an allergic reaction. Based on recognition of these signs and symptoms, the nurse or his or her designee will be able to give treatment and medication.

Medication policies vary from school to school. Some schools restrict all medications to the nurse's office. Obviously, this could be a potential problem if the nurse's office is situated a long distance from the eating areas. Death from anaphylaxis can potentially occur minutes after exposure. Ideally, the cafeteria monitors will be equipped with epinephrine in such a set-up. Other schools have the students' medications in a fanny pack that is handed off from one teacher to the next as the student changes classes. Most schools allow students to carry their epinephrine and asthma inhalers after age ten to twelve, with the written permission of their physician.

It is important for families to provide a **written action plan** to the school and school nurse. You should develop this individualized plan with your physician. It can be a one-page sheet with the following information:

- **Student's name** and **personal information**
  age, class, address, home and emergency phone numbers, parents' names and emergency phone numbers, closest relatives or designees from the family to act in the parents' absence
- **Physician's name** and **phone number**
- **Medical information**
  specific diagnoses, including history of asthma
  specific allergies
  all medications
- **Signs and symptoms of an allergic reaction**
  **Skin:** itching, flushing, hives, swelling
  **Mouth:** itching and swelling of the lips, tongue, mouth
  **Throat:** itching, swelling, tightness of throat, difficulty swallowing, difficulty speaking, hoarseness, cough
  **Chest:** cough, chest pain or tightness, shortness of breath, wheezing
  **Heart:** weak, thready pulse; dizziness; passing out
  **Abdomen:** nausea, vomiting, diarrhea, abdominal pain and cramps
- **Action plan**
  1. If peanut product is ingested and only mild skin symptoms are observed, give (*antihistamine, dose*). If hives are severe or rapidly progressive, give EpiPen/EpiPen Jr./Twinject0.3 mg/0.15 mg.

2. If systemic symptoms or anaphylaxis occurs, give EpiPen/EpiPen Jr./Twinject0.3 mg/0.15 mg.
3. Call emergency contacts (Mother/Father/Designee).
4. Call physician.
5. Call ambulance, if emergency contacts or physician not reachable.

This action plan can be modified for the individual student according to his or her specific history and needs. It needs to be revised as the medical history changes and should be updated at least at the beginning of each new academic year. A copy of this action plan should be kept with the epinephrine. FAAN's Emergency Health Care Plan is a convenient form, reproduced here, that can be used as a template for your child's written action plan. You can also download it from FAAN's Web site at www.foodallergy.org.

---

### Personalize Your Child's Items

Pasting the child's photograph on the Action Plan sheet as well as to the child's EpiPen prescription box for the school nurse makes for easy and quick identification in an emergency situation. Another good idea is to have the younger child eat on a placemat that has his name, photograph, and diagnosis of "peanut allergy" on it, to further minimize the possibility of mistakes. Printing companies can make stickers on which you can print your child's name, picture, and "peanut allergy." These stickers can very useful in labeling medications, lunch and goodie bags, placemats, and other items.

---

## Food Allergy Action Plan

**Student's**
**Name:**_____D.O.B:_____Teacher:_____

**ALLERGY TO:**_____

Asthmatic Yes* ☐ No ☐ †Higher risk for severe reaction

> Place
> Child's
> Picture
> Here

### ◆ STEP 1: TREATMENT ◆

**Symptoms:**

**Give Checked Medication**:
(To be determined by physician authorizing treatment)

| | | | |
|---|---|---|---|
| • | If a food allergen has been ingested, but *no symptoms*: | ☐ Epinephrine | ☐ Antihistamine |
| • Mouth | Itching, tingling, or swelling of lips, tongue, mouth | ☐ Epinephrine | ☐ Antihistamine |
| • Skin | Hives, itchy rash, swelling of the face or extremities | ☐ Epinephrine | ☐ Antihistamine |
| • Gut | Nausea, abdominal cramps, vomiting, diarrhea | ☐ Epinephrine | ☐ Antihistamine |
| • Throat† | Tightening of throat, hoarseness, hacking cough | ☐ Epinephrine | ☐ Antihistamine |
| • Lung† | Shortness of breath, repetitive coughing, wheezing | ☐ Epinephrine | ☐ Antihistamine |
| • Heart† | Thready pulse, low blood pressure, fainting, pale, blueness | ☐ Epinephrine | ☐ Antihistamine |
| • Other† | _____ | ☐ Epinephrine | ☐ Antihistamine |
| • | If reaction is progressing (several of the above areas affected), give | ☐ Epinephrine | ☐ Antihistamine |

The severity of symptoms can quickly change. †Potentially life-threatening.

### DOSAGE

**Epinephrine:** inject intramuscularly (circle one) EpiPen® EpiPen® Jr. Twinject™ 0.3 mg Twinject™ 0.15 mg
(see reverse side for instructions)

**Antihistamine:** give_____
                                                    medication/dose/route

**Other:** give_____
                                            medication/dose/route

### ◆ STEP 2: EMERGENCY CALLS ◆

1. Call 911 (or Rescue Squad: _____ ) . State that an allergic reaction has been treated, and additional epinephrine may be needed.

2. Dr. _____ at _____

3. Emergency contacts:
Name/Relationship                    Phone Number(s)

a. _____    1.)_____   2.) _____

b. _____    1.)_____   2.) _____

c. _____    1.)_____   2.) _____

EVEN IF PARENT/GUARDIAN CANNOT BE REACHED, DO NOT HESITATE TO MEDICATE OR TAKE CHILD TO MEDICAL FACILITY!

Parent/Guardian Signature_____    Date_____

Doctor's Signature_____    Date_____
                                (Required)

Reprinted with the permission of The Food Allergy & Anaphylaxis Network, 11781 Lee Jackson Hwy, Suite 160, Fairfax, VA 22033-3309.

## What can parents do for the school?

Michael's mother became very involved with the school as a result of her son's peanut allergy. She started by talking to his class and answering questions about peanut allergy and how it affected Michael. She then talked to parents about peanut allergy at PTO meetings. She joined the local chapter of AAFA (Allergy and Asthma Foundation of America) and attended their meetings. She subsequently organized lectures and speakers and arranged special programs for the students and parents of Michael's school.

---

The most important part of any plan is communication and education, and here is where the family has a responsibility to the school. Entering kindergarten and first grade are big landmarks in your child's life. This is the ideal time to establish the educational messages that you as parents will ultimately be responsible. Most problems that you and your child will encounter result from ignorance. Therefore, before school begins, meet with the principal and your child's teacher to discuss his or her specific needs as well as your suggestions for educating the class about peanut allergy. Find out whether the school has had students with similar allergic conditions and whether they have had experience dealing with medical emergencies. You and your child can do an informal presentation to the class. Contact the Food Allergy & Anaphylaxis Network (FAAN) about their School Food Allergy Program; it provides an in-depth discussion for parents and school staff with a food awareness plan. There is also an excellent videotape available from FAAN (see Appendix A) called "Alexander, The Elephant Who Couldn't Eat Peanuts," aimed at elementary school children.

You can also offer to educate school staff, teachers, and other personnel with an in-service presentation. Also invite the other parents. Consider inviting your pediatrician or allergist to be a part of this educational session. I have gone to schools to speak with school

## Questions You Need to Ask the School

- Does the school have a full-time nurse? If not, what days is he or she there and who has the responsibility for administering medical care in his or her absence?
- Is the student allowed to carry the epinephrine?
- What plan do you have in place in the event of a medical emergency?
- How many peanut- or food-allergic students have you had experience with? Are there any currently enrolled?
- Has the school ever dealt with an anaphylactic reaction? What was the outcome?
- What is the closest hospital to which a sick student would be transported?
- Is the cafeteria peanut-free? Would you provide a peanut-free zone?
- If my child is the victim of a bully or harassment, how would you deal with that problem?
- Can we as parents set up an educational forum or discussion group to help educate students, teachers, and staff about peanut allergy?

nurses, teachers, and students about allergies. Often, the child's physician might be able to provide the in-service teaching as well. I have done so on numerous occasions and find it very useful for educating my patients, their families, and school staff, and also for helping my management by improving communications, especially with the school nurse. The school nurse can be the "eyes and ears" for the physician and can be one of his or her most useful allies in caring for patients.

## How will this allergy affect my child's emotional and social development?

Michael, age seven, has had a lifelong history of peanut allergy, as well as allergies to tree nuts, dairy products, and eggs. At age five, he had a severe anaphylactic reaction at a birthday party, most likely to nuts. He eats school lunch in a special "allergy-free" room separate from the main cafeteria.

He also has asthma, which requires him to use multiple medications during school hours. He dislikes gym and has refrained from participating in team sports. He is constantly teased by classmates and is called "Peter Pan" and the "peanut man." Michael's parents are concerned that he is withdrawing and is depressed, and they are consulting a psychologist to counsel him.

---

One of the more difficult challenges of having a child with a serious and potentially fatal medical problem is the general lack of knowledge that he or she will encounter in the other students and their families. Most people don't understand how dangerous food allergies can be. They also tend to be unaware of the concepts of hidden allergens, cross contamination, and the fact that very small amounts of an allergenic food can do as much harm as the amount normally eaten at a meal.

People feel imposed upon when they have to make personal concessions to situations they do not fully comprehend. They may feel that you are "overprotective" when you ask that peanuts be removed from your child's environment. Therefore, education of the child's classmates and their families is just as important as the education of the school and its staff. This can be accomplished in many ways, both in the classroom and outside school. Meeting face to face with people is generally the most effective way of achieving cooperation. You can arrange to be on the agenda for the next PTO meeting, invite parents to the classroom setting, or meet in the school cafeteria, where some of these potential problems can be made more obvious.

Besides lack of knowledge and ignorance, the other common problem many children face is that of teasing and harassment. Being "different" is likely to make youngsters the target of harassment by other children, and food allergy can easily make your child the prey of a bully. Unfortunately, there have been many instances of peanut-allergic children not only being teased but also being physically threatened by other children. There was an example of a bully thrusting an open jar of peanut butter in the face of someone with peanut allergy. The life-threatening potential of this situation makes it more serious than just dealing with another bully, and the consequences are much more severe than just hurt feelings. This behavior must be dealt with in a swift, definitive way, directly with the school principal. Again, a face-to-face meeting with the offending child's family might be the way to stop this behavior. Many children are unable to comprehend death, and life-threatening scenarios may be too abstract for them to understand, so they don't realize the consequences of their actions and behavior.

Another consequence of having a serious and potentially fatal medical problem, such as peanut allergy, is in the fear and anxiety that it generates. Particularly in children, phobias toward eating can result, especially if the child has already experienced a severe allergic reaction. It is important that the child understand that, while being careful is good, once safe foods are identified, they can be eaten without fear. Most fears in an older child can be overcome with patience, understanding, and reasoning. In young children, fear can be overcome with support and with the child knowing that there is always someone there to help if he or she gets sick. Your child's teacher, school nurse, and principal can be your surrogates during school hours; familiarizing these persons not only with your child's medical needs but also with his or her specific fears will give your child confidence in them and ultimately enable him or her to develop self-confidence.

Because some schools have their food-allergic students sit at special "allergy- or peanut-free tables," these children are separated from their friends and often feel isolated and even punished. Friendships and relationships often suffer as a result. However, many loyal friends will bring peanut-free lunches so they can sit at the table. Again, appropriate education of all involved is the most effective way to prevent problems.

Children often use their medical problems as an attention-getting device, and food allergies are no exception. They may claim that they are experiencing active symptoms such as "trouble breathing," "throat closing," "chest pain or tightness," "abdominal pain," and "uncontrollable itching" caused by their allergies. It is important to address these symptoms early on and to recognize whether they are truly allergic reactions. You have to be certain that there was actual peanut exposure associated with these symptoms. Physical signs of an allergic reaction are important in documenting a true allergic reaction. The presence of redness, rash, hives, and swelling can be helpful. Substantiate symptoms that involve breathing difficulties and asthma with a measurement of lung function with a peak flow meter. You must bear in mind however, that anaphylaxis need not always present with these symptoms, so the severity and urgency of each episode needs to be carefully evaluated by someone with expertise, such as the school nurse. If the attention-getting symptoms are rewarded with attention, your child may develop a behavior pattern that will make it very difficult to evaluate future reactions that are genuinely a result of peanut exposure. Professional counseling should be considered if your child's food allergy problem is complicated by this issue.

### What are some of the problems unique to the peanut-allergic adolescent?

Jennifer, age sixteen, has had peanut allergy since age four and has not had any problems with restricting peanut and peanut products. She had a recent allergic reaction when her new boyfriend kissed her after eating peanut butter candy, and she developed facial hives. She is very upset today because her boyfriend doesn't seem to understand the seriousness of her allergy and has announced that he shouldn't have to "put up with this" and is breaking up with her. She "wishes she would die and be over with this."

---

In addition to all the previously discussed issues, the adolescent presents a unique set of problems. We're all too familiar with the mood swings and occasional rebellious "acting out" behavior of teenagers. Adolescents tend to seek some measure of control and a feeling that they can be independent. Many adolescents express this by deliberate actions to test the limits that have previously been set for them. For the food-allergic adolescent, this may sometimes take the form of either denial or rejection of their allergic condition and ignoring the restrictions placed on them. Such seemingly self-destructive behavior in adolescents is a common problem observed for the entire range of medical problems, from diabetes to asthma to smoking, as well as drug and alcohol abuse.

Adolescents value belonging to their peer group and will try to avoid being cast as "different." They may feel embarrassed telling a new friend, particularly if they may feel attracted to that friend, of medical problems such as a food allergy, which might limit where they could go out and have fun. For all of the above reasons, the teenage years are actually when more anaphylaxis occurs from accidental exposures. A helpful approach might be to involve friends and peers who might share similar medical problems, as well as the adolescent's personal physician or anyone else he or she trusts and respects. Giving the adolescents as much responsibility and control of their lives as possible will reinforce the feeling of trust and confidence they need as they reach for adulthood.

For the at-risk adolescent who already has a tendency toward eating disorders, being on a restricted diet and avoiding food for medical reasons may worsen this problem. Again, early recognition of these issues and early counseling will help prevent them from escalating. Blatantly self-destructive behavior or evidence of eating disorders clearly warrants consultation with a professional counselor.

I have found that a number of my patients who did well through high school had their first accidental exposures and anaphylaxis during freshman year of college. This is usually the first time your child will be completely independent and has to make choices and decisions without you close by. In a new environment that includes new eating places with no food-allergy restrictions, new friends, and new temptations, it can be difficult for the previously sheltered child to make the transition.

Just as adolescence is the time to prepare socially, emotionally, physically, and intellectually for eventual adulthood, it is also the time for food-allergic adolescents to prepare to be on their own and to be able to deal with their allergies independently. Certainly, high school is the time to begin this preparation by giving them gradual control. By the time your adolescent is ready to go off to live alone, he or she should be ready for independent living. When looking at colleges in the junior and senior years of high school, visit campuses and inquire about the food services, as well as about health services and the infirmary. Once the college has been selected, consult the local allergist so that he or she knows your child in the event of a problem. Meet the medical staff, and show them your emergency action plan. Forward your child's medical records, especially those of your allergist.

### Should I wear a Medic-Alert bracelet?

The Medic-Alert bracelet is a metal tag engraved with an individual's name and vital information in case of emergency, usually the diagnosis/allergies and brief instructions. The tag can be worn as a bracelet around the wrist or on a chain around the neck. Its purpose is to provide life-saving information in case the patient is unable to give it. In addition, the responding person can call the Medic Alert's 24-Hour Emergency Response Center, which has a computerized data file on the person, with medical history and other vital information.

Obviously, in the event of loss of consciousness due to an anaphylactic reaction, a passerby can be immediately informed of the patient's diagnosis by reading the Medic-Alert bracelet and, if so instructed, administer life-saving epinephrine. Whether a peanut-allergic patient chooses to wear the Medic-Alert bracelet depends on the risk of fatal anaphylaxis and the risk of the patient being incapacitated to the point where he or she is incapable of self-administering the epinephrine or communicating with other people. The use of the Medic-Alert bracelet in very young children would be for the remote possibility of their being left alone without adult supervision. A young child should always be under the supervision of a responsible adult well-versed in the child's specific allergic condition and management of an allergic reaction, including the use of epinephrine.

Of greater concern is the young child who is not quite old enough to understand and articulate the specific problem but is just old enough that he or she might not always be under constant adult supervision. This is the child at the greatest risk for an accidental ingestion, often resulting from sharing and playing with other children. This age group is usually the late preschool to early elementary school grade level. Generally, older children and adults do not have any of these issues, and the main reason for wearing the Medic-Alert bracelet would be in case of encountering a situation where loss of consciousness or incapacity occurs. The Medic-Alert bracelet comes in several sizes and styles and can be fairly unobtrusive. You can obtain ordering information from your doctor or contact Medic-Alert directly by calling (800) 432-5378 or writing to 2323 Colorado Avenue, Turlock, CA 95382.

# CHAPTER 7

# PREVENTION OF PEANUT AND OTHER FOOD ALLERGIES

### Should I avoid peanuts and other allergenic foods during pregnancy?

Jill had a craving for peanut butter during her first pregnancy and admitted that every chance she had, she ate peanut butter sandwiches and peanut butter spread on crackers, cookies, and fruit. Her love for peanut butter continued through the three-month period she nursed her baby. Gregory, now two, developed peanut-allergy symptoms the very first time he was exposed, with hives on his mouth and face. Jill just found out that she is pregnant again, and she wants to know whether she should eliminate peanut products from her diet.

There is evidence that the fetus has the capability of making immune responses; specifically, it can make IgE responses to milk and egg proteins, as well as to some environmental allergens. There are two studies that examine the effect of avoiding allergenic foods during pregnancy on the development of food allergies and allergic disease in infancy. Maternal avoidance and elimination diets did not prevent the development of allergic diseases, including food allergy, in either study.

In spite of these findings, however, the British Medical Council has recommended the avoidance of peanuts and peanut products by all pregnant and nursing women with newborns at high risk for allergies. These potentially allergic babies would have either personal or family histories of allergies, asthma, or eczema. This recommendation may have been influenced by Hourihane's 1997 study, which shows that there is a relationship between increased maternal consumption of peanuts during pregnancy and lactation and earlier onset of peanut allergy in infancy and childhood. The increasing numbers of peanut-allergic individuals, as well as the permanence of peanut allergy, are also factors to consider in making this recommendation. Although there are no guarantees, giving up peanuts during the time of pregnancy and breast feeding could potentially prevent your child from experiencing this life-threatening allergy.

### Is breast feeding helpful in preventing food allergies?

Ellen's first baby was bottle fed with infant formula. He was colicky in the first two weeks and needed several formula changes until things got better with a soy formula. At age two months, he developed eczema at about the same time that foods were added to his diet. He was diagnosed with milk, egg, and peanut allergy by the pediatrician, with positive RAST tests at age six months. He wheezed for the first time at age ten months when he had viral bronchiolitis. Since that time, he has wheezed with colds and respiratory infections. He is now three and wheezes with active play and running. His pediatrician feels that he has asthma. Ellen is pregnant with her second child and asks whether breast feeding this baby will help prevent what her son had to go through.

---

Breast feeding in the first year of life is recommended by most pediatricians and by the American Academy of Pediatrics. Human breast milk is nutritionally complete and contains everything the newborn and infant needs to grow and develop. Breast milk also contains numerous components of the immune system that help the baby defend against infection. These include protective antibodies, which increase natural immunity, and various enzymes that can kill bacteria, in addition to other protective elements of the immune system. Because of these benefits, all babies should be nursed, regardless of their risk for allergic disease.

Because allergic diseases—which include not only food allergy but allergic rhinitis (hay fever), asthma, and eczema—are all genetic and inherited, the baby who has relatives with these allergic diseases is at a greater risk for developing them. If one of your parents has allergies, your chances of developing allergies is about 33 percent. If both of your parents have allergies, your chances of developing allergies is about 66 percent. For the infant with the genetic risk factors for being allergic, many specialists have recommended exclusive breast feeding for the first six months. The important aspect of breast milk with regard to allergies is that no other foods need to be given with it, so the exclusively breast-fed infant is not exposed to numerous "foreign" proteins that may be sensitizing. If the nursing mother is able to avoid eating allergenic foods such as peanuts, tree nuts, and shellfish, the baby's exposure to sensitizing proteins is even less.

The newborn and infant gastrointestinal tract is a very complex system that must be capable of breaking down and absorbing foreign nutrient proteins, while at the same time rejecting and fighting foreign bacterial and viral proteins that are harmful to the body. If, because of immaturity, the baby's GI tract is ineffective in modifying and processing the allergenic aspects of these food proteins, inflammatory and allergic reactions to these proteins can result, causing the baby to become sensitized to them. If you follow a "hypoallergenic" diet while breast feeding exclusively in this critical first six months, exposure to foreign proteins and allergens is significantly reduced, and the likelihood of developing food allergies is lessened. Despite its intuitive and theoretical appeal, however, there are no placebo-controlled studies to show that this strategy is effective in preventing the development of childhood food allergies.

No one knows exactly at what age the gastrointestinal tract has matured enough to be able to adequately process and handle foreign proteins without significant risk of sensitization. In general, many experts feel that by age three years, the child's GI tract is able to handle most allergenic foods and is therefore at a reduced risk for developing food allergies. For this reason, the American Academy of Pediatrics now recommends that children with the most risk factors for being allergic to foods (having a personal history and/or family history of allergies, asthma, and eczema) be restricted from the highly allergenic foods, such as peanuts, tree nuts, and shellfish, until after the age of three.

### What is a reasonable schedule for the introduction of foods into the diet of a potentially food-allergic infant?

There are no universal recommendations or policies with regard to this question. Based on available information from studies, most allergists would recommend strict breast feeding for at least four to six months. There is some controversy in regard to this advice, but I would suggest that the mother restrict highly allergenic foods from her diet, including peanuts, tree nuts, and shellfish, to minimize the risk of sensitization through breast milk.

Nursing supplements or weaning can be done with an elemental or hypoallergenic formula such as Neocate, Elecare, Nutramigen, Pregestimil, or Alimentum. These products are available in most pharmacies and many supermarkets. Solids should be delayed until age six months and should start with the least allergenic foods first, such as rice cereal, fruits, and vegetables. Individual foods should be added sequentially, weekly or biweekly, one food at a time. Animal proteins, which are more allergenic, should come after the fruits and vegetables. The American Academy of Pediatrics (2000) recommends to hold off on cow's milk and dairy until age twelve months and eggs until age twenty-four months. Highly allergenic foods, such as peanut, tree nuts, and shellfish, should ideally be held off until after age three years. Some conservative recommendations would hold off on the introduction of peanuts and nuts until age five years.

| Age to introduce food | Food |
| --- | --- |
| Birth to 4–6 months | Breast milk |
| 4–6 months | Rice cereal, fruits, and vegetables* |
| 6–12 months | Wheat, oat, cereal grains, soy, chicken, turkey, beef, lamb, pork* |
| 12 months | Milk |
| 24 months | Egg |
| 36 months–5 years | Peanut, tree nuts, fish, shellfish |

*Introduce individual foods sequentially, one food per week.

# CHAPTER 8

# THE FUTURE OF PEANUT ALLERGY

**Can peanut allergy be treated with allergy shots?**

Allergy shots, or allergen immunotherapy, has been in use for the treatment of hay fever and asthma since the early 1900s. This form of treatment works by inducing an immunity to the various environmental allergens, such as pollens, molds, dust mites, and animals, by regular monthly injections of the allergenic material in graded minute amounts over a period of three to five years. Since the 1970s, allergen immunotherapy has been successfully used in the treatment of insect-sting anaphylaxis from honeybees, yellow jackets, hornets, and wasps by the administration of minute amounts of insect venom over five years or more.

For patients meeting the selection criteria, the success rate of immunotherapy for hay fever is as high as 80 percent, with the possibility of long-term remission of symptoms. The success rate for venom immunotherapy is even higher, at 90 to 95 percent, effectively curing this potentially fatal allergy. Usually, the main side effects of immunotherapy are allergic reactions localized to the site of the injection, but occasionally systemic reactions, such as hives, runny nose, cough, wheezing, and anaphylaxis, do occur.

## Immunotherapy for food allergy

The use of immunotherapy for food allergy was first reported by Freeman in 1930. He was able to desensitize a seven-year-old boy who had unstable asthma triggered by fish ingestion, as well as hives, angioedema (swelling), vomiting, and diarrhea, with fish exposure. The patient lost both his fish-allergic reactions and his skin test reactivity to fish. He was able to maintain his desensitized condition by eating fish and taking cod liver oil every day.

There were almost no subsequent reports of treatment of food allergy with immunotherapy in the following decades because the standard treatment for food allergy continues to be avoidance and an elimination diet. In 1987, Dr. John Carlston, of Eastern Virginia Medical School, published on the successful treatment of two patients with food allergies with food immunotherapy. The first patient had peanut allergy with anaphylaxis, including allergic symptoms caused by inhalation of peanut odor. She was treated with injections of peanut extract, starting at a dose of 0.05 ml of a 1:100,000 weight per volume dose. The dose was gradually increased 150-fold to a maintenance dose of 0.5 ml of a 1:2,000 dose. This maintenance dose is the equivalent of 1/10th of a teaspoon of a solution made by mixing 1 gram of peanut in 2 liters (more than 2 quarts) of water. This is a minuscule amount of peanut! She had frequent allergic reactions to treatment, including wheezing, but she did lose her peanut sensitivity. After a year of symptomless peanut exposures, her immunotherapy was stopped. She continued to do well on follow-up one year later.

The second patient reported was a seafood restaurant worker whose asthma was exclusively triggered by her working environment. She was treated with a mixture of fish (cod, flounder, halibut, mackerel, and tuna) and shellfish mix (clam, crab, scallop, oyster, and shrimp), and her asthma improved greatly, allowing her to work without symptoms. She was also able to eat shrimp without any problems.

Then, in 1992, Drs. Nelson and Leung and their colleagues at the National Jewish Hospital in Denver, Colorado, published a randomized placebo-controlled study of peanut immunotherapy in patients with a history of peanut allergy and anaphylaxis. Eleven patients began the protocol; eight patients reached maintenance immunotherapy. Of the four patients finishing the study, three patients received peanut immunotherapy and one received placebo. The three patients who received peanut immunotherapy had a significant decrease in symptoms on DBPCFC and a decrease in skin test reactivity to peanut. The placebo-treated patient had no change in either DBPCFC or skin test reactivity. Unfortunately, systemic reactions occurred at the very high rate of 13.3 percent, almost four times that of pollen immunotherapy. The systemic reactions were all mild to moderate; there were no anaphylactic reactions in the three patients. This study is the first to demonstrate in a well-controlled manner, that traditional immunotherapy can be an effective treatment for food allergy and anaphylaxis, dispelling the old dogma that immunotherapy for food is ineffective.

Presently, immunotherapy for food is still considered experimental because of the high incidence of side effects and the lack of larger, more extensive controlled studies documenting safety of the treatment.

## What does the future hold for
## the treatment of peanut allergy?

There are presently many exciting areas of research in food allergy. Better understanding of the immunology of allergic reactions, as well as progress being made in identifying and characterizing peanut allergens with gene sequencing, may one day make it possible to manipulate the immune response to these allergens and, perhaps, to "turn off" the allergic response.

### Treatment That Decreases IgE

One approach is to decrease the amount of circulating IgE in the patient. Antibodies to IgE can be made, which will bind to and remove IgE from the circulation. Because the presence of IgE is required for all allergic reactions, this solution theoretically could be the answer to all types of allergic diseases, from food allergies to hay fever to eczema to asthma. These anti-IgE antibodies have already been studied in mice with good results, and several human trials in patients with hay fever and asthma show promising early results. Omalizumab (Xolair) was the first anti-IgE antibody approved for the treatment of moderate to severe asthma in June 2003. It is administered by subcutaneous injection every two to four weeks.

In 2003, Drs. Nelson and Leung at the National Jewish Hospital in Denver, and Dr. Sampson's group in New York, published a multicenter study examining the effects of TNX-901, an anti-IgE vaccine, in eighty-one patients, ages thirteen to fifty-nine years old, with severe peanut allergy and histories of anaphylaxis. On average, these patients could not eat more than half a peanut before experiencing allergic reactions and anaphylaxis. After receiving injections of anti-IgE vaccine for three months, they were able to tolerate up to nine peanuts without reacting at all.

This type of treatment may be able to prevent reactions from the common types of accidental exposures occurring in restaurants and in cross-contaminated foods and reduce the frequency of anaphylaxis. Although the original anti-IgE vaccine reported in 2003 is no longer available, Xolair, a similar anti-IgE vaccine available for the treatment of moderate to severe asthma, is currently being studied for the prevention of peanut anaphylaxis in both children and adults by the same investigators.

### DNA Vaccine and Peptide Therapy

Another novel approach to treatment is a DNA vaccine, which contains the DNA coding for peanut allergen Ara h2. Injection of this

DNA induces a suppressive immune response that "turns off" the response to Ara h2, thus preventing any allergic reaction to peanut. This approach successfully reduced peanut anaphylaxis in mice and may be applied to humans in the near future.

The main drawback to traditional immunotherapy with peanut extracts is the very high rate of both local and systemic allergic reactions to each injection. There is certainly a risk of anaphylaxis as well if an incorrect dose is given or an error is made in the administration. To avoid this problem, the immunotherapy material can use peanut protein that has been modified to contain only the portion that is recognized by the patient's immune system (called **epitope**) and to not have the portion that will bind to IgE on mast cells (called **peptide**). With the injection of this material, the immune system will be able to generate the same type of immunity to peanut without any chance for allergic reactions to the injections. This type of immunotherapy has been called **peptide therapy** and has already been successfully studied in human trials with cat allergen and ragweed pollen allergen. Hopefully peanut peptide immunotherapy will be tested in the future.

**Treatment Based on the Hygiene Hypothesis**

Using the principles of the Hygiene Hypothesis, which theorizes that the immune system turns "allergic" because it has not been stimulated with enough bacterial infections, scientists working with animal models have actually tried to "turn off" allergic immune systems with bacterial proteins. Some scientists have found that, by using certain heat-killed bacteria combined with modified peanut proteins, peanut anaphylaxis could be prevented in peanut-allergic mice. Dr. Xiu-Min Li and her colleagues at the Mount Sinai Medical Center in New York have found success administering this combination as a rectal preparation in mice. They are hoping to study it in humans as well.

Another approach that uses the principles of the Hygiene Hypothesis is to have allergic individuals take probiotics, which are "good bacteria." Probiotics, such as lactobacillus acidophilus found in yogurt, lactobacillus GG, and bifidobacteria, are sold without prescription. They are commonly used to treat diarrhea caused by antibiotic use. Generally considered safe products, they are classified as supplements and not considered pharmaceuticals. There are ongoing studies examining their effectiveness in preventing eczema and other allergic diseases, such as asthma and hayfever. Probiotics have not been studied for peanut allergy. So far, there is no evidence that food allergies are prevented by using probiotics. You may wish to consult your doctor about this approach.

### Nonallergic Food Through Genetic Engineering

A different approach to the problem of food allergy is to make the food itself nonallergenic, or hypoallergenic, through genetic engineering. Characterization of the three peanut allergens Ara h1, Ara h2, and Ara h3 has identified the portions of peanut protein that bind to IgE. This binding of the peanut allergens to IgE triggers the mast cells to release histamine and the other chemical mediators that cause allergic symptoms and anaphylaxis. Without binding of IgE to the peanut allergens, no allergic reaction would occur.

That said, because the genetic structure and sequence of the three major peanut allergens is known, scientists are now able to alter the peanut proteins and render them incapable of binding to IgE. Through genetic engineering, a new type of peanut that contains these altered proteins could be grown; these peanuts would not trigger any allergic reactions in peanut-allergic patients. Genetically engineered plants have already been available for years now, with qualities such as resistance to pests and disease, enhanced nutritional content, longer shelf life, and many other desirable features. Preliminary studies by Dodo and coworkers show successful transformation of Georgia green peanut varieties with a modified Ara h2 protein. They are now growing these genetically modified hypoallergenic peanut plants to maturity and seed formation and will eventually be able to test these new peanut strains for their allergenic activity.

## Chinese Herbal Medicine

Recently, Dr. Li and her colleagues at Mount Sinai Medical Center in New York have studied the effectiveness of Chinese herbal medicines in preventing peanut anaphylaxis in peanut-allergic mice. The Chinese have used herbal medicines for centuries to treat a variety of diseases, including allergies and asthma. Dr. Li purified the crude herbal mixtures and applied the treatment to her peanut-allergic mice. Mice sensitized to peanuts were treated with a formula of nine traditional Chinese herbs twice daily for seven weeks. The mice treated with placebo herbs all developed anaphylaxis when challenged with peanuts, while none of the mice treated with the herbal formula had any allergic symptoms for as long as five weeks following completion of treatment.

The treated mice had lower levels of peanut-specific IgE, which suggests a possible mechanism of action for the herbs. There were no observed side effects in the treated mice. Eventually, Dr. Li plans to study the effectiveness of her Chinese herbal formula for peanut allergy in humans. This research may eventually lead to a safe, easy-to-take oral treatment of peanut allergy that already has been used for centuries in traditional Chinese medicine.

# WHERE CAN I LEARN MORE ABOUT FOOD ALLERGIES?

The best single source of information on food allergies is your local allergy specialist. He or she has the special training to help clarify your various symptoms and to diagnose specific allergies. Most importantly, he or she can give specific recommendations on allergy-control measures and avoidance strategies and can give you the most current treatment based on the newest advances in allergy and immunology research. He or she will work with your primary care doctor to formulate a well-thought-out and reasonable plan for managing your food allergies.

For the best resource available to the public on food allergies, the Food Allergy & Anaphylaxis Network (FAAN) is unparalleled. This nonprofit organization serves "to increase public awareness about food allergies and anaphylaxis, to provide education, and to advance research on behalf of all those affected by food allergies." The organization was founded by Anne Muñoz-Furlong, whose daughter was diagnosed with milk and egg allergies as an infant. Lack of information and support for people and families with food allergies prompted her to form this organization, which in addition to being the best resource for patients and families, is also involved in funding and conducting research and educational programs. It is very active in the food and restaurant industry and in government and legislative issues. FAAN formed the National Registry of Peanut and Tree Nut Allergy for all peanut- and nut-allergic people to register and provide information about their allergy history. They also now have a National Registry of Shellfish Allergy. These registries provide a valuable database from which numerous important medical studies have originated.

FAAN is online at www.foodallergy.org. Their address is 11781 Lee Jackson Hwy, Suite 160, Fairfax, VA 22033-3309, and their telephone number is (800) 929-4040. They publish a bimonthly newsletter, *Food Allergy News,* for adults and a separate one for children. They also have many publications on specific topics, including peanut allergy, tree nut allergy, and understanding food labels; a useful cookbook; and recipes in every newsletter. They have excellent school programs as well as instructional videotapes, including one I highly recommend: "The Elephant Who Couldn't Eat Peanuts." One of their most useful services to patients is their issuance of "Special Allergy Alert Notices," which keeps the public up to date on the food industry's latest news bulletins, recalls, and warnings on products. I recommend FAAN to all my patients with food allergies.

Other sources of information on food allergies, or allergic diseases in general, are the Allergy and Asthma Foundation of America (AAFA), the American Academy of Allergy, Asthma and Immunology (AAAAI), and the American College of Allergy, Asthma and Immunology (ACAAI). AAFA provides educational programs to the general public and local support groups for patients and families with asthma and allergic diseases, including food allergies.

Although AAAAI and ACAAI are professional organizations for allergy and asthma specialists, they do provide information and educational materials to the general public on asthma and all allergic diseases. They also have a referral directory so that patients can be given names of allergy and asthma specialists in their local communities. Both organizations have Web sites and can be found at www.aaaai.org and www.acaai.org, respectively.

# WHAT ARE THE MAIN TAKE-HOME POINTS TO REMEMBER ABOUT PEANUT ALLERGY?

- Peanuts are one of the main causes of food allergies and, together with tree nut allergies, are the leading cause of fatal and near-fatal food anaphylaxis.
- The incidence of peanut and tree nut allergy in children has doubled over the past five years.
- Most people do not outgrow peanut allergy (only 20 percent do), unlike most other food allergies. Of those who do outgrow peanut allergy, 9 percent can relapse and become allergic again.
- The symptoms of allergic reactions are itching; hives; swelling of face, throat, and tongue; abdominal pain; vomiting and diarrhea; difficulty breathing; wheezing; dizziness; loss of consciousness; and shock.
- Anaphylaxis is a systemic reaction that can lead to cardiovascular collapse and death. It requires immediate treatment with epinephrine.
- Because there is not yet a cure for peanut allergy, strict avoidance is the key to management.
- Accidental ingestions are a fact of life; 25 percent of peanut-allergic patients have had accidental ingestions and reactions in the past year.
- Be prepared to deal with accidental ingestion and anaphylaxis when eating and traveling outside the home. The peanut-allergic individual should have epinephrine (EpiPen or Twinject) on his or

her person wherever contact with food is expected, especially outside the home. He or she also should have a rapid-acting liquid antihistamine, such as diphenhydramine (Benadryl).

- Create a written action plan with your physician, keeping a copy for yourself and filing another with the medical office at the workplace or nurse's office in school.
- Learn to read labels and ingredient lists.
- Be aware of the problem of hidden allergens, cross contamination, and indirect exposures.
- When eating outside the home, inform people of your allergy, especially food servers, restaurant staff, school cafeteria staff, airline staff, and so forth.
- Peanut oil may not be safe if it has been contaminated through cooking or if it is crude, cold-pressed, or unrefined.
- Peanut allergy is caused by a specific immunologic response to peanut protein.
- Peanut allergy is usually genetically determined and inherited.
- Peanut allergy is more common in an individual who has other allergic diseases such as hay fever, asthma, or eczema, and it is more common in close relatives, such as siblings, parents, and other relatives, of those who have allergic diseases.
- Parents with allergic diseases will have children at higher risk of developing allergic disease, including food allergy.
- Confirm the allergy by consulting with an allergist, who can evaluate the problem with allergy testing.
- The gold standard for the diagnosis of food allergy is the double-blinded placebo-controlled food challenge (DBPCFC).
- Potentially allergic infants should be breast fed for the first six months of life to minimize exposure and sensitization to food proteins. Ideally, the maternal diet should not contain highly allergenic foods such as peanuts, tree nuts, and seafood.
- The highly allergenic foods such as peanuts, tree nuts, and seafood should be withheld from the potentially allergic child's diet until

after age three years. In general, this appears to be the approximate age at which the child's immune system and gastrointestinal tract is able to handle and process these highly allergenic foods.

• Knowledge of the molecular structure of peanut allergens may allow for development of novel vaccines to treat peanut allergy. Advanced biotechnological techniques may lead to new strains of genetically engineered peanuts that do not cause allergic reactions.

• Until then, education, increased public awareness, and prevention remain the principal approaches to this increasingly common problem.

# GLOSSARY OF TERMS

**Allergen** A substance that causes an allergy; in the case of food, it is usually a protein.

**Allergic Rhinitis** An allergic condition characterized by nasal congestion, itching, sneezing, and mucous, usually caused by environmental allergens. Commonly called "hay fever," which is a misnomer because patients don't get a fever and the allergen is not hay.

**Allergy** An abnormally high sensitivity to certain substances, such as food, pollen, medications, or insect stings.

**Anaphylaxis** A severe, rapidly progressive, potentially fatal systemic allergic reaction characterized by hives, swelling, difficulty breathing, wheezing, and gastrointestinal symptoms. **Anaphylactic shock** is characterized by a drop in blood pressure, in addition to the aforementioned symptoms, and is life threatening.

**Angioedema** Swelling of tissue. When angioedema occurs in a critical area, such as the throat or tongue, it can obstruct breathing and be life-threatening.

**Antibody** A protein produced in response to foreign substances, such as bacteria, toxins, and allergens. Antibodies are essential elements of the immune system as it responds; they also cause allergic reactions. The antibodies that neutralize bacteria and viruses are IgG and IgM. The antibody produced in allergic reactions is **IgE.**

**Antihistamine** A drug that counteracts the effects of **histamine** by binding to **histamine receptors** on tissues. This characteristic makes it important in treating allergies of all types because histamine causes the symptoms of allergic reactions.

**Asthma** A chronic inflammatory condition of the lungs, resulting in difficulty breathing, cough, chest tightness, and wheezing. It is commonly triggered by infection, allergy, and physical factors such as exercise and cold air temperature.

**Atopic Dermatitis** The medical term for **eczema.**

**B Cell** A white blood cell that produces antibodies such as **IgE.**

**Bronchospasm** Spasms of the airways in the lung, causing obstruction that results in the symptoms of **asthma.**

**Casein** A white, tasteless, odorless milk protein. It is the basis of cheese and is also used to make adhesives, plastics, and paint.

**Conglutin** One of the allergenic peanut proteins.

**Cross-reaction** The reaction between an allergen and IgE generated against a different but similar allergen, often belonging to the same family or category. For example, a person who is allergic to walnuts and experiences anaphylaxis to pecans has had a cross-reaction between walnuts and pecans.

**DBPCFC** Double-blind placebo-controlled food challenge, which is the gold standard for diagnosing food allergy. In this procedure, neither the person tested nor the doctor (hence double blind) will know whether the placebo or the actual food is given. This procedure helps eliminate bias from the study.

**Eczema** A chronic inflammatory skin condition, often associated with allergic triggers such as food or environmental allergens. It is more common in people and their relatives who also have asthma and allergic rhinitis.

**Elemental Diet** A prepared, nutritionally complete **hypoallergenic** diet consisting of basic nutrients such as amino acids, fatty acids, and simple sugars and containing no allergenic proteins. It is in liquid form and available for infants, children, and adults.

**Elimination Diet** A diet that has strictly and completely eliminated the specific food(s) you are allergic to. Children who adhere to their elimination diet are more likely to outgrow their food allergy.

**Epinephrine** The drug of choice for anaphylaxis, which relieves the skin, cardiovascular, gastrointestinal, and respiratory symptoms of an acute allergic reaction.

**EpiPen** Automatic injector of the drug epinephrine; used to treat anaphylaxis.

**Epitope** The part of the food protein that is recognized by the immune system and targeted by antibodies such as IgE.

**Gluten** The main allergenic protein in wheat, also found in rye and barley.

**Glycinin** One of the allergenic peanut proteins.

**Glycoprotein** Any protein containing a carbohydrate sugar component. Most allergenic proteins are glycoproteins.

**Histamine** A physiologically active chemical released by **mast cells** as part of the allergic reaction. Histamine causes all the symptoms of allergy, such as itching, sneezing, swelling, mucous production, and wheezing. The actions of histamine are blocked by antihistamine medications.

**Hydrolysate** The product of hydrolysis, a chemical reaction that breaks down and degrades a chemical or food, such as soy or milk hydrolysate. Hydrolysates are not necessarily less allergenic than the parent compound.

**Hypoallergenic** Having a decreased potential to cause allergic reactions.

**IgE** The antibody, produced by B cells, that recognizes allergens.

**Immunology** The study of the structure and function of the immune system.

**Immunosuppression** Suppression of the immune system by drugs, by radiation, or by diseases such as malignancies and AIDS. When the immune system is suppressed, it no longer performs many of its functions, such as recognizing the difference between self and nonself and fighting bacteria and viruses.

**Intolerance** An adverse reaction to food that is not mediated by the immune system. In gastrointestinal intolerances, it is due to an inability to digest certain foods (e.g., lactose intolerance).

**Lactalbumin** One of the **whey** proteins in milk.

**Lactoglobulin** The other whey milk protein.

**Mast cell** The cell of the immune system that produces histamine and other chemical mediators involved in allergic reactions. IgE attached to mast cells will bind to specific allergens, causing the mast cell to release **histamine.** Mast cells are found in all the target organs of allergic symptoms, such as skin, eyes, nasal mucous membranes, sinuses, ears, lungs, blood vessels, and the gastrointestinal tract.

**Mediators** Chemicals made by cells of the immune system that *mediate* various reactions in the body such as allergic reactions.

**Ovalbumin** An egg-white protein.

**Ovomucoid** An egg-white protein.

**Peptide Therapy** A form of allergy therapy that involves injections of only the active allergic component (which is called the peptide) of the allergic protein. The theoretical advantage of this form of allergy injection is that there are many fewer allergic reactions and side effects to the injections.

**Placebo** A substance that contains no active ingredient. It is used in medical studies as a control for patients who believe that they are being given the active ingredient.

**RAST (RadioAllergoSorbent Test)** A blood test that measures the level of **allergen**-specific **IgE** in your blood to determine whether you are allergic to that allergen. It is almost as accurate as a skin test.

**Receptor** A molecular structure or site on the surface of a cell that is able to bind to chemicals, such as **histamine,** or to proteins, such as antibodies like **IgE.**

**Skin Prick Tests** Skin tests are performed by pricking a pointed instrument or device through a drop of allergenic extract that has been placed on your skin. The skin is not broken; the prick enables enough fluid extract to penetrate the first layer of the skin. An allergic skin reaction comparable to a small mosquito bite will form if you are allergic to that allergen. Skin prick tests are a reliable way to diagnose allergies.

**Tropomyosin** A muscle protein that is the main allergen in shellfish.

**Twinject** Automatic injector of the drug epinephrine; used to treat anaphylaxis.

**Urticaria** The medical term for **hives:** a skin rash characterized by very itchy red welts usually caused by exposure to an allergen.

**Vicilin** An allergenic peanut protein.

**Whey** The watery part of milk that separates from the curds (also known as **casein**) when milk curdles. Whey contains **lactalbumin** and **lactoglobulin.**

# REFERENCES

The references I have cited throughout this book are listed below, for those of you who wish to go to the primary sources. In addition to the sources below, *Food Allergy News* (FAN), the newsletter of the Food Allergy & Anaphylaxis Network, is an invaluable reference source. A compilation of all the peanut-allergy articles previously published by FAAN is also available.

American Academy of Pediatrics Committee on Nutrition. "Hypoallergenic infant formulas." *Pediatrics* 2000; 106:346-9.

Bernhisel-Broadbent, J, and H Sampson. "Cross-allergenicity in the legume botanical family in children with food hypersensitivity." *J Allergy Clin Immunol* 1989; 83:435-440.

Bock, SA, et al. "Double-blind, placebo-controlled food challenge (DBPCFC) as an office procedure: A manual." *J Allergy Clin Immunol* 1988; 82:986-97.

Bock, SA. "The natural history of food sensitivity." *J Allergy Clin Immunol* 1982; 69:173-77.

Bock, SA. "The natural history of peanut allergy." *J Allergy Clin Immunol* 1989; 83:900-904.

Bock, SA, et al. "Fatalities due to anaphylactic reactions to foods." *J Allergy Clin Immunol* 2001; 107:191-3.

Brown, SGA. "Clinical features and severity grading of anaphylaxis." *J Allergy Clin Immunol* 2004; 114:371-6.

Buford, JD, and JE Gern. "The hygiene hypothesis revisited." *Immunol Allergy Clin N Am* 2005; 25:247-62.

Burks, W, et al. "Peanut allergens." *Allergy* 1998; 53:725-30.

Carlston, JA. "Injection immunotherapy trial in inhalant food allergy." *Annals Allergy* 1988; 61:80-82.

De Montis, G, et al. "Sensitisation to peanut and vitamin D oily preparations." *Lancet* 1993; 341:1411.

Dodo, H, et al. "A genetic engineering strategy to eliminate peanut allergy." *Curr Allergy Asthma Reports* 2005; 5:67-73.

Ewan, P. "Clinical study of peanut and nut allergy in 62 consecutive patients: New features and associations." *Brit Med J* 1996; 312:1074-78.

Ewan, P. "Prevention of peanut allergy." *Lancet* 1998; 352:4-5.

Fleischer, DF, et al. "The natural progression of peanut allergy: Resolution and the possibility of recurrence." *J Allergy Clin Immunol* 2003; 112:183-9.

Fleischer, DF, et al. "Peanut allergy: Recurrence and its management." *J Allergy Clin Immunol* 2004; 114:1195-201.

Fleischer, DF, et al. "The natural history of tree nut allergy." *J Allergy Clin Immunol* 2005; 116:1087-93.

Food Anaphylaxis Task Force of Massachusetts. "Managing Life Threatening Food Allergies in Schools." Malden, MA 2002. Massachusetts Department of Education. www.doe.mass.edu/cnp.

Fries, J. "Peanuts: Allergic and other untoward reactions." *Annal Allergy* 1982; 48:220-226.

Goetz, DW, et al. "Cross-reactivity among edible nuts: Double immunodiffusion, crossed immunoelectrophoresis and human specific IgE serologic surveys." *Ann Allergy Asthma Immunol* 2005; 95:45-52.

Hourihane, J. "Peanut allergy-current status and future challenges." *Clin Experimental Allergy* 1997; 27:1240-1246.

Hourihane, J. "Peanut allergy: Recent advances and unresolved issues." *J Royal Society Med* 1997; 30 (suppl):40-44.

Hourihane, J, et al. "An evaluation of the sensitivity of subjects with peanut allergy to very low doses of peanut protein: A randomized, double-blind, placebo-controlled food challenge study." *J Allergy Clin Immunol* 1997; 100:596-600.

Hourihane, J, et al. "Peanut allergy in relation to heredity, maternal diet, and other atopic diseases; results of a questionnaire survey, skin prick testing, and food challenges." *Brit Med J* 1996; 313:518-21.

Hourihane, J, et al. "Randomised, double blind, crossover challenge study of allergenicity of peanut oils in subjects allergic to peanuts." *Brit Med J* 1997; 314:1084-1088.

Hourihane, J, et al. "Resolution of peanut allergy: Case-control study." *Brit Med J* 1998; 316:1271-5.

Hourihane, J. et al. "Resolution of peanut allergy following bone marrow transplantation for primary immunodeficiency." *Allergy* 2005; 60:536-7.

James, J. "Airline snack foods: Tension in the peanut gallery." *J Allergy Clin Immunol* 1999; 104:25-27.

Jones, RT, et al. (abstract). "Recovery of peanut allergens from ventilation filters of commercial airliners." *J Allergy Clin Immunol* 1996; 97:423.

Kelso, JM (Letter) "A second dose of epinephrine for anaphylaxis: How often needed and how to carry." *J Allergy Clin Immunol* 2006; 117:464-5.

Klemola, T, et al. "Feeding a soy formula to children with cow's milk allergy: The development of immunoglobulin E-mediated allergy to soy and peanuts." *Pediatr Allergy Immunol* 2005; 16:641-6.

Koerner, C, and T Hays. "Nutrition basics in food allergy." *Immunol Allergy Clin NA* 1999; 19:583-603.

Korenblat, K, et al. "A retrospective study of epinephrine administration for anaphylaxis: How many doses are needed?" *Allergy Asthma Proc* 1999; 20:383-6.

Lack, G, et al. "Factors associated with the development of peanut allergy in childhood." *N Engl J Med* 2003; 348:977-85.

Legendre, C, et al. "Transfer of symptomatic peanut allergy to the recipient of a combined liver-and-kidney transplant." *N Engl J Med* 1997; 337:822-3.

Lehrer, S et al. "Immunotherapy for food hypersensitivity." *Immunol Allergy Clin N Am* 1999; 19:563-81.

Leung, D, et al. "Effect of anti-IgE therapy in patients with severe peanut allergy." *N Engl J Med* 2003; 348:986-93.

Li, X, "Beyond allergen avoidance: Update on developing therapies for peanut allergy." *Curr Opin Allergy Clin Immunol* 2005; 5:287-92.

Lieberman, P. "Biphasic anaphylactic reactions." *Ann Allergy Asthma Immunol* 2005; 95:217-226.

Loza, C, and J Brostoff . "Peanut allergy." *Clin Exp Allergy* 1995; 25:493-502.

McIntyre, CL, et al. "Administration of epinephrine for life-threatening allergic reactions in school settings." *Pediatrics* 2005; 116:1134-40.

Mulherin, K. "Day care center sued for discriminating against food-allergic children." *Food Allergy News* 1997; 6(3):3.

Muñoz-Furlong, A. "Food labeling rules, practices and changes to come." *Food Allergy News* 1996; 5:3.

Muñoz-Furlong, A. "Daily coping strategies for patients and their families." *Pediatrics* 2003; 111:1654-61.

Muñoz-Furlong, A. "Food allergy in schools: concerns for allergist, pediatricians, parents and school staff." *Ann Allergy Asthma Immunol* 2004; 93(suppl 3):S47-S50.

Nowak-Wegrzyn, A, and HA Sampson. "Food allergy therapy." *Immunol Allergy Clin N Am* 2004; 24:705-725.

Oppenheimer, J, et al. "Treatment of peanut allergy with rush immunotherapy." *J Allergy Clin Immunol* 1992; 90:256-62.

Perry TT, et al. "Distribution of peanut allergen in the environment." *J Allergy Clin Immunol* 2004; 113:973-6.

Plaut, M. "New directions in food allergy research." *J Allergy Clin Immunol* 1997; 100:7-10.

Rawas-Qalaji, MM, et al. "Sublingual epinephrine tablets versus intramuscular injection of epinephrine: Dose equivalence for potential treatment of anaphylaxis." *J Allergy Clin Immunol* 2006; 117:398-403.

Rix, K, et al. "A psychiatric study of patients with supposed food allergy." *British J Psychiatry* 1984; 145:121-26.

Rosen, J, et al. "Skin testing with natural foods in patients suspected of having food allergies: Is it a necessity?" *J Allergy Clin Immunol* 1994; 93:1068-1070.

Sampson, H. "Food allergy. Part 1: Immunopathogenesis and clinical disorders." *J Allergy Clin Immunol* 1999; 103:717-28.

Sampson, H. "Food allergy. Part 2: Diagnosis and management." *J Allergy Clin Immunol* 1999; 103:981-9.

Sampson, H. "Food allergy and the role of immunotherapy." *J Allergy Clin Immunol* 1992; 90:151-2.

Sampson, H, et al. "Fatal and near-fatal anaphylactic reactions to food in children and adolescents." *N Engl J Med* 1992; 327:380-4.

Sampson, H. "Managing peanut allergy." *Brit Med J* 1996; 312; 1050-1.

Sampson, H. "Peanut allergy." *N Engl J Med* 2002; 346:1294-9.

Sampson, H, et al. "Second symposium on the definition and management of anaphylaxis: Summary report—Second National Institute of Allergy and Infectious Disease/Food Allergy & Anaphylaxis Network symposium." *J Allergy Clin Immunol* 2006; 117:391-7.

Shreffler, WG, et al. "Microarray immunoassay: association of clinical history, in vitro IgE function, and heterogeneity of allergenic peanut epitopes." *J Allergy Clin Immunol* 2004; 113:776-82

Sicherer, S, et al. "Clinical features of acute allergic reactions to peanut and tree nuts in children." *Pediatrics* 1998; 102(1). URL:www.pediatrics.org/cgi/content/full/102/1/e6.

Sicherer, S, et al. "Genetics of peanut allergy: A twin study." *J Allergy Clin Immunol* 2000; 106:53-6.

Sicherer, S, et al. "Prevalence of peanut and tree nut allergy in the U.S. determined by a random digit dial telephone survey." *J Allergy Clin Immunol* 1999; 103:559-62.

Sicherer, S., et al. "Prevalence of peanut and tree nut allergy in the United States determined by means of a random digit dial telephone survery: A 5-year follow-up study." *J Allergy Clin Immunol* 2003; 112:1203-7.

Sicherer, S, et al. "Self-reported allergic reactions to peanut on commercial airliners." *J Allergy Clin Immunol* 1999; 103:186-9.

Sicherer, S. "Clinical update on peanut allergy." *Ann Allergy Asthma Immunol* 2002; 88:350-61.

Sicherer, S, and H Sampson. "Food allergy." *J Allergy Clin Immunol* 2006; S470-5.

Simons, E, et al. "Can epinephrine inhalations be substituted for epinephrine injections in children at risk for systemic anaphylaxis?" *Pediatrics* 2000; 106:1040-44.

Simons, E, et al. "Epinephrine for the out-of-hospital (first aid) treatment of anaphylaxis in infants: Is the ampule/syringe/needle method practical?" *J Allergy Clin Immunol* 2001; 108:1040-44.

Skolnick, HS, et al. "The natural history of peanut allergy." *J Allergy Clin Immunol* 2001; 107:367-74.

Smith, AF. "Peanuts: The illustrious history of the goober pea." University of Illinois Press, Chicago, 2002.

Steinman, H. " 'Hidden' allergens in foods." *J Allergy Clin Immunol* 1996; 98:241-250.

Teuber, S, et al. "Allergenicity of gourmet nut oils processed by different methods." *J Allergy Clin Immunol* 1997; 99:502-7.

Vadas, P, et al. "Detection of peanut allergens in breast milk." *JAMA* 2001; 285:1746-8.

Webb, L, et al. (abstract) "Anaphylaxis: A review of 593 cases." *J Allergy Clin Immunol* 2004; 113:S240.

Weeks, R. "Peanut oil in medications." *Lancet* 1996; 348:759-60

Wood, R. "More answers to commonly asked questions about anaphylaxis." *Food Allergy News* 1999; 8:6.

Wensing, M, et al. "The distribution of individual threshold doses eliciting allergic reactions in a population with peanut allergy." *J Allergy Clin Immunol* 2002; 110:915-20.

Yunginger, J. "Lethal food allergy in children." *N Engl J Med* 1992; 327:421-2.

Yunginger, J, et al. "Fatal food-induced anaphylaxis." *JAMA* 1988; 260:1450-52.

Zeiger, R. "Prevention of food allergy in infants and children." *Immunol Allergy Clin N Am* 1999; 19:619-646.

# ABOUT THE AUTHOR

Michael C. Young, M.D., is Assistant Clinical Professor of Pediatrics at Harvard Medical School and practices at Children's Hospital, Boston, and at South Shore Allergy & Asthma Specialists in South Weymouth, MA. He is a graduate of Harvard University and Yale Medical School. He trained in pediatrics and allergy and clinical immunology at Children's Hospital in Boston. Dr. Young is a past president of the Massachusetts Allergy Society and has been selected for inclusion in *The Guide to Top Doctors* by the Center for the Study of Services and by *Best Doctors in America*. He has received honors from the Allergy & Asthma Foundation of America and the Food Allergy & Anaphylaxis Network.

Dr. Young is also a member of the Massachusetts Department of Education Task Force on Anaphylaxis, which developed the first guidelines in the country for the management of food allergies and anaphylaxis in schools. In addition to scientific and medical journal articles, Dr. Young also wrote the chapter on management of anaphylaxis in the textbook *Pediatric Allergy, Principles and Practice*.